Practical Points
on Boat
Engines

Practical Points on Boat Engines

HANS DONAT

Nautical

First published in Great Britain 1979 by
NAUTICAL PUBLISHING COMPANY LIMITED
Lymington, Hampshire SO4 9BA
in association with George G. Harrap & Co. Ltd.,
London

ISBN 0 245 53333 8

Filmset and printed in Great Britain by
BAS Printers Limited, Over Wallop, Hampshire

Contents

Introduction

In these pages, I discuss the main features of the most common engines found in boats and yachts. The book is laid out so that the reader can interest himself either in just the engine alone, or in the entire installation, whatever the size and type of his boat.

Both diesel and petrol engines are covered, though diesel is gaining afloat as lighter motors are produced. Despite higher initial cost for equivalent power, safety, running costs and environmental factors favour the diesel.

The four-stroke cycle is shown below, and sketches in the early part of the book show typical engines and instruments. In what follows I have tried to cover those points that would not be found in a general book on automobile engines. As well as the engine itself, the quality of a boat's machinery depends on whether the engine has been properly converted for marine use and is suitable for the boat, and whether the correct transmission has been chosen. The common difficulties for amateurs have been dealt with, so that problems with engines will be minimized and they can then relax to enjoy other aspects of sailing and motor boating.

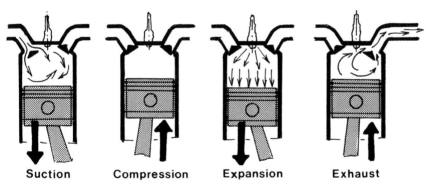

| Suction | Compression | Expansion | Exhaust |

The inboard engines covered in this book all work on the four-stroke principle. From l. to r.: suction through the open inlet valve (petrol engine—air and fuel; diesel engine—air). The mixture is compressed by the rising piston and is ignited just before top dead centre (diesel—fuel ignites at the moment of injection). The working stroke follows and, finally, the burnt gases are forced out through the open exhaust valve into the exhaust manifold.

1. Engine considerations and comparisons

The buyer of a series-produced boat has no opportunity to specify the optimum combination of boat and power unit, but has to rely on the designer. It will help considerably if he can spot a reliable and well matched combination.

Different criteria prevail for series-produced boats than for one-off construction, because the former must be marketable and this has disadvantages as follows, the typical motor sailer, for instance has:

- far too small a propeller, and is frequently offered with power output adequate for anything from a planing boat to a displacement boat.
- Always supposing that he has any choice at all the purchaser can only choose between two makes of engine.
- Of the remaining boats in which a petrol engine is to be installed, very few are so designed that a diesel engine could replace the standard petrol engine.

Development in engine building, and diesels in particular, has made such strides that the power to weight ratio of modern diesels is fully competitive with that of petrol engines of the sixties. This has overcome the greatest problem that discouraged the use of diesel engines in fast motor boats of relatively short waterline length.

Generally speaking the intention to sell motor cruisers in large numbers results in their being built to designs which logically only perform at their best over a narrow power range, and they are often over-powered at the risk of safety or are under-powered lame ducks. Anyway, as will be obvious to anyone with an open mind, a boat designed for low speeds cannot possibly have better characteristics at high speed than a boat which has been designed for high speeds from the first, just as no-one will win a Formula 1 motor race driving a tractor.

Many errors are made even when the engine is used purely for auxiliary purposes. The most common causes of shortcomings in performance are poor installation and inadequate engine compartment ventilation, incorrect propeller measurements, too small a propeller and too little down-gearing of engine speed between the engine and the propeller which results in poor efficiency.

A propeller of given measurements can only work with a high degree of efficiency within a certain limited range of revolutions and, unless this range is used, the best of engines is worthless because the engine power delivered to the shaft is not converted into thrust but is dissipated in the water.

How can a boat buyer resolve these problems? How can he find his way through the confusion of theory and sales talk? To form an opinion on an engine based on the materials of which it is made is virtually impossible, and one must rely on the fact that an engine manufacturer would not continue long in business if poor materials were used. This can best be explained by an example. Sea water resistant aluminium alloy is very difficult to cast because the alloy does not flow particularly well. If silicon and copper are added the molten metal flows into complicated dies, filling them completely. Rejection of spoiled castings is almost entirely avoided, but the engines are unusable after two years use at sea.

There are many figures which can be used when comparing engines, as well as the more valuable figures obtained from brake tests.

It would be quite wrong to consider the engine in isolation. A marine engine is only as good as the entire installation.

It is doubtful, anyway, whether sufficient attention is paid to the engine when a boat or sailing yacht is bought because, often not unreasonably, the buyer feels that the yard will have already considered which engine is best for the boat. On the other hand a good builder need not necessarily be an engine expert. The manufacturer's guarantee will be taken over, the engine serviced by the local service agency, the propeller measurements 'expertly' but roughly estimated and the engine installed, generally by the yard.

None of this is easy, but I will try in what follows to introduce you more fully to the engine—that thing that lies beneath the cockpit floor and causes all the vibration!

What is a marine engine?

Over a period of some years engine building has reached such a high technical level that no sudden advance or breakthrough can be expected. Progress continues over details, and performance and reliability improve although the length of working life may suffer. Engine makers have different aims from those of the sixties, such as reduction in air pollution by exhaust fumes, and lower fuel consumption.

Well-known companies have withdrawn from racing, neither for economic reasons nor for lack of interest, but because the racing engine can no longer contribute to the continued development of the engine for normal use. Commercial development trends lead to rationalization and, consequently, to standardization and larger scale production. The result is that, today, very few marine engines exist that were designed as such. The 'solid' types of marine engines still on sale can be recognized by their large size and excessive weight, and externally because the flywheel is forward. Engines used in boats today are generally vehicle or industrial engines converted for marine use.

Naturally the question arises immediately—does an automobile engine or the engine of a concrete mixer make a good boat engine? The answer is short and clear:

● Yes, provided that it has a closed cooling circuit or a double cooling circuit, is appropriately governed, and has a water-cooled exhaust manifold.

● If direct (salt water) cooling is used all material that comes into contact with sea water must be resistant to salt water and to the corrosive effect of polluted rivers.

In other words, if a good car engine is scrupulously converted for marine

9

boat engines

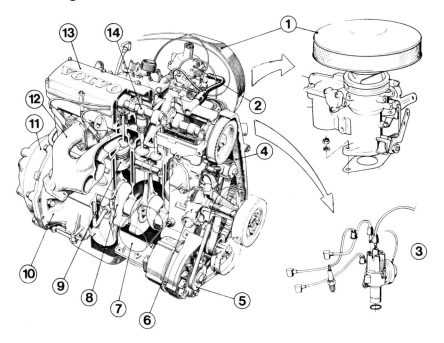

Main components of the petrol engine:

1. Air filter
2. Carburettor
3. Ignition system
4. Toothed camshaft drive belt
5. Alternator
6. Cooling water pump
7. Oil filter cartridge
8. Crankshaft
9. Piston
10. Cylinder black with wet liners (not exchangeable)
11. Flywheel housing
12. Exhaust manifold (must be water-cooled for marine engines)
13. Rocker box
14. Camshaft with overhead valves

purposes and is properly installed it will also be a good boat engine.

Even if an engine were designed specifically for marine work today, it would not look so very different, nor be made of different materials, and the main problem that concerns engines used in pleasure craft would still be — corrosion while the engine lies idle. This is a problem that can only be resolved by maintenance and care, whatever the engine.

So it is that our marine engines are the converted cousins of engines used in motor cars, lorries, dredgers, tracked vehicles, cranes, tractors and concrete mixers. Anyone who considers that this ancestry reduces the value should reflect that engines used on land work far longer hours in more arduous conditions than would ever normally be met in boats used for pleasure.

It is only thanks to the immense investment in commercial engine production that the diesel engines of the late seventies almost match the normal petrol engine as to power-to-volume ratio size, and power-to-weight ratio—or at any rate those of petrol engines made in the late sixties.

Converting engines for marine purposes (marinizing)

Naturally a vehicle or industrial engine cannot be installed in a boat just as it is. It has to be converted first. Various points have to be considered according to its intended application on land, and these will decide whether it will be a good boat engine. The most important alterations are as follows:

1. The cooling water of a vehicle engine is recooled in a cellular radiator. This is impossible in a boat if overlarge ducts and overpowerful ventilators are to be avoided. Either the coolant in the engine cooling circuit has to pass through a heat exchanger where it is recooled by seawater, the two circuit cooling system, or the coolant passes through keel coolers in a closed cooling circuit. The only exception is when the engine is made of metal that is suitable for direct raw water cooling, but this is extremely rare in modern engines.

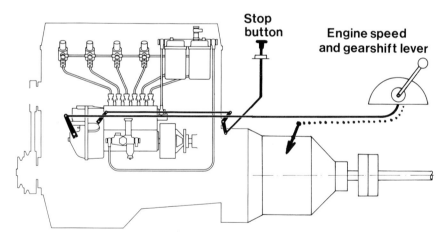

Stop button

Engine speed and gearshift lever

Whereas the speed of a petrol engine is controlled by the butterfly valve in the carburettor, that of the diesel engine is controlled by the quantity of fuel delivered. The engine speed control lever is connected to a toothed control rod in the fuel injection pump by a push-pull cable, and the control rod regulates the fuel delivery plungers. The petrol engine is stopped by switching off the ignition. The diesel, having no ignition system, is stopped by operating a stop button or lever which either reduces the quantity of fuel delivered to nil, or opens a decompression port in the cylinder head.

boat engines

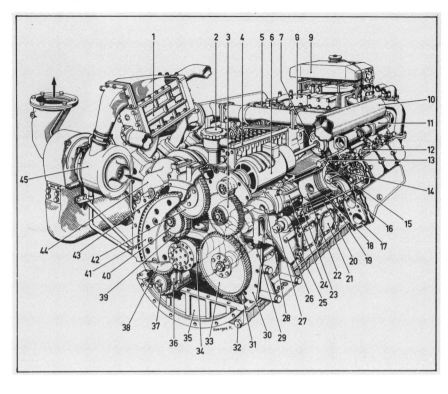

Main components of a diesel engine:
The figure shows a Deutz water-cooled vee engine with pre-combustion chambers, supercharger and aftercooling. The fuel, cooling, lubrication and exhaust systems are discussed in the section on engine installation.

1. Aftercooler
2. Crankcase ventilation
3. Intermediate gear
4. Fuel injection pump
5. Double fuel filter
6. Alternator
7. Coupling piece for centrifugal pump
8. Oil cooler
9. Water recooler
10. Combustion air intake manifold
11. Coolant outlet line
12. Injection valve
13. Glow plug
14. Rocker

23. Tappet
24. Connection rod
25. Main bearing screw
26. Oil feed line
27. Right hand camshaft
28. Crankshaft
29. Main bearing screw
30. Baffle plate
31. Oil suction pump
32. Sump drain plug
33. Camshaft drive gear
34. Crankshaft gear
35. Sump
36. Pressure oil pump
37. Oil pump drive gear

12

15. Pre-combustion chamber
16. Exhaust valve
17. Exhaust manifold
18. Wet liner
19. Coolant inlet line
20. Pushrod
21. Inspection plate
22. Piston

38. Camshaft drive gear
39. Large intermediary gear
40. Small intermediary gear
41. Flywheel with rim gear
42. Fuel injection pump gear
43. Starting pinion
44. Starter motor
45. Exhaust turbo-supercharger

Furthermore vehicle engines have a pressure cooling circuit and, if direct cooling were fitted, the inevitable result would be a reduction in working temperature and, therefore, greater wear on the cylinder walls.

Even if there is no pressure, circuit care is needed because an engine block made of sea water resistant metal, in conjunction with fittings made of other metals, can lead to severe corrosion problems in the cooling circuit lines when there is too great a difference between the sea water temperatures at the cooling water intake and outlet.

If you have read instruction manuals for vehicle engines carefully you will know that they recommend that cooling water should be as soft as possible, and that antifreeze should be added to permit the water to remain in the engine throughout the winter. This is valid for boat engines too.

2. The exhaust of a vehicle or industrial engine is not cooled. In the narrow and poorly ventilated engine compartment of a boat this would lead
   ● to increased danger of fire and explosion because the exhaust would start to get red hot.
   ● The temperature in the engine compartment would also rise so much that power output would decrease until the engine became useless, while rubber and synthetic materials would be weakened.

This means that the exhaust manifold must be suitably insulated, or be provided with a water jacket which extends to the point where the temperature of the exhaust gases has been reduced sufficiently for the material and surroundings by injecting cold water into the gases.

3. The shape of the sump sometimes has to be altered so that the engine is properly lubricated, even when the engine is lying at an angle. This relates particularly to those modern engines which are mounted across a motor car at an angle of up to 30° but which will be installed upright in the boat. The design of the vehicle engine sump with pressure feed lubrication (splash lubrication is no longer used) is such that it is generally suitable for use in a boat. In some cases an oil recooler is necessary.

Those are the three main points.

Other components have to be adapted: gearbox, flywheel, starter motor and alternator both have to be earthed and protected from water, sometimes two alternators are needed to provide adequate generating capacity, exhaust system, fuel lines (filter and shut-off valves), flexible coupling (torque).

boat engines

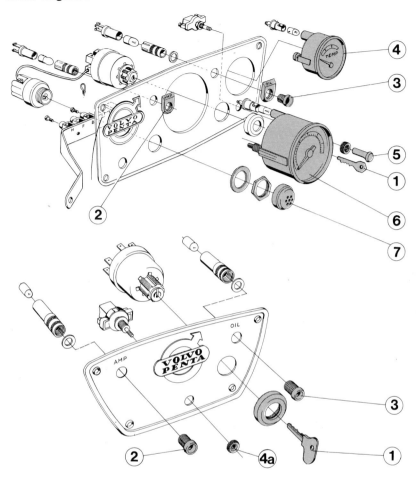

Monitoring instruments: The controls vary considerably in number according to the type and output of the engine. In principle an engine can be monitored adequately if a water temperature guage and an oil pressure gauge are fitted. Two types of instrument panel in general use are illustrated, one for motor boats above and one for sailing boats below:

1. Ignition key
2. Battery charging warning light
3. Oil pressure warning light
4. Cooling water temperature gauge
4a Cooling water temperature
   warning light

5. Switch
6. Revolution counter, tachometer
7. Acoustic alarm signal for oil
   pressure and cooling water
   temperature (much
   recommended)

14

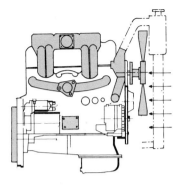
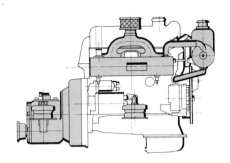

Mercedes Benz OM 615 diesel engine as used in the Mercedes automobile 220D

Marine WM 54 engine with Hurth HBW 15 gears, based on the Mercedes OM 615

Technical specification

Technical specification

Water-cooled vehicle diesel engine, four cylinders, vertical

Water-cooled marine diesel engine, four cylinders, vertical

Vehicle rating*	44 kW (60 hp)	Yacht rating*	40 kW (54 hp)
Rev/min	4,200	Rev/min	3,300
Bore	87 mm	Bore	87 mm
Stroke	92·4 mm	Stroke	92·4 mm
Swept volume	2·197 dm³	Swept volume	2·197 dm³
Weight		Weight	
(vehicle engine)	200 kg	(dry with gearbox)	256 kg
Length (inc. radiator)	720 mm	Length	1,068 mm
Breadth	650 mm	Breadth	618 mm
Height	790 mm	Height	701 mm

Comparison of a vehicle diesel and a marine diesel, based on the same Mercedes Benz OM 615 engine.

The areas shaded grey are the main parts that have to be converted. Further details will be found on the next pages.

boat engines

Right: the main parts that have to be altered when converting a vehicle or industrial engine for marine use. The Mercedes OM 615 is used as an example. 1 = water-cooled exhaust manifold with connection to heat exchanger. 2 = heat exchanger and mountings. 3 = water pump with mountings and connections. This is an additional water pump which serves the second cooling circuit. 4 = oil cooler with flanges and pipes. An oil cooler is often an additional requirement in boats; on land the oil in the large capacity sump is cooled adequately by the vehicle's own speed. 5 = bell housing, gearbox. 6 = gearbox mountings. 7 = torsion damper which connects the engine to the gearbox. 8 = flexible engine mountings. 9 = reverse and reduction gear. 10 = air filter. In many cases no conversion is required. 11 = sump. Latterly this has been so designed, for commercial vehicles and industrial engines at any rate, that it can also be used for marine engines. The air filter here is the same as the one fitted to the commercial vehicle, whereas the car engine on the previous page has a different filter and also a different air intake manifold. The sump, too, can be used for either version.

Conversion parts can also be obtained from motor retailers (the engine from a car involved in an accident), and also from specialist conversion kit suppliers.

The list of parts for converting the OM 615 offers the alternatives of fitting either a closed fresh water circuit cooled by a separate raw water cooling circuit (A) or a closed circuit (B).
In A: 1 = seawater inlet. 2 = seawater filter. 3 = additional cooling water pump for the recooling circuit. 4 = heat exchanger in which the engine coolant is recooled. 5 = seawater outlet.
In B: 1 = cooling pipe below the hull. 2 = circulating pump, identical to the seawater pump left. 3 = heat exchanger case which does not recool but serves merely as a header tank. 4 = pipe leading to the symmetrically fitted second keel pipe. 5 = second keel cooling pipe. 6 = connecting pipe to first cooling tube which completes the circuit. The area required for cooling is much smaller than used to be thought necessary (see p. 89).

16

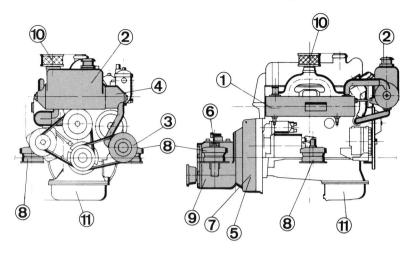

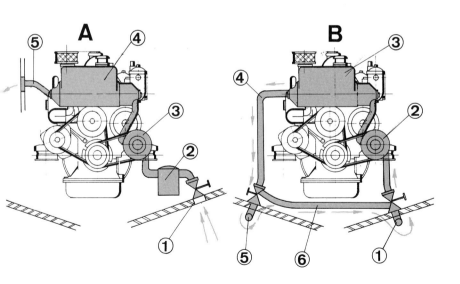

17

boat engines

This list could be extended to cover many details, but the individual points are covered in greater detail later.

After all this has been dealt with the engine still has to be installed correctly because the best of engines will not perform well if, for example, the air supply is inadequate.

Details of converting an engine for marine purposes is shown opposite.

● About 30–60% of the cost of a new marine engine can be saved by converting a second-hand vehicle engine yourself and buying the parts required. This naturally calls for a considerable amount of skill and should not be attempted by the inexperienced.

Petrol (gasoline) versus diesel

The question as to whether to carry petrol (gasoline) or diesel oil on board must always be answered in favour of diesel oil on the grounds of safety. Flash point is the point at which a liquid gives off vapours which, in the case of fuel, mix with air and can explode. The flash point of petrol is below 0°C whereas that of diesel oil is over 55°. Furthermore the price of diesel is generally lower throughout the world. This statement is basically correct and is only affected by prices being increased in some countries by mineral oil companies and governments.

Unfortunately these are not the only factors that influence the choice because the engines that use these fuels are so different. It is easiest to make comparisons by using the table below which has been set out to indicate which is preferable (e.g. purchase price 'lower' is entered on the petrol engine side).

Although some petrol-engined boats with membrane carburettors, fuel injection and electronic ignition are very reliable and safe the risk is inherent in the fuel itself. If these 'safe' petrol engines are installed particular care has to be taken over maintenance and regular replacement (every two years) of fuel lines, membranes etc.

The general principle is clear although, undoubtedly, particulars of certain products somewhat alter the picture. This evaluation can be proved by technical specifications and figures such as those in the table on page 19.

Fortunately the problem is less complicated than it would appear. Recent technical advances have resulted in a diesel engine with a power to weight ratio which, purchase price apart, make it ever more attractive, even for installation in light planing boats. This is why the cases when petrol engines have to be installed on account of weight become ever fewer. There remains only the very

	Petrol	Diesel
Purchase price	lower	
Length of working life		longer
Cost of fuel		lower
Safety (fuel)		greater
Reliability in use		greater
Weight, volume	smaller	
Noise	less	
Pollution (exhaust)		less

Values for comparing petrol and diesel engines

	Petrol	Diesel
Fuel (flash point)	under 0°C	over 55°C
Cost of fuel	100%	about 80%
Power range (kW)	220	220
Revolutions per minute	4,000–6,500	2,000–5,000
Swept volume (litre or dm³)	up to 7	up to 15
Power to volume ratio (kW/1)	10–45(50)	8–22(30)
Power to weight ratio (kg/kW)	2–10	4–25
Specific fuel consumption (g/kWh)	380–270	300–220
Specific fuel consumption (1/kWh)	0·52–0·37	0·36–0·27
Specific fuel consumption (gals/kWh)	0·11–0·08	0·08–0·06
Compression ratio	7–10:1	16–24:1

Comparison of the more important criteria affecting petrol and diesel engines.

high initial cost of a diesel which certainly cannot be paid off as quickly in a boat as in a motor car. It is nevertheless very interesting to compare them as to this point, based on the power of your engine.

Air cooling or water cooling
The question as to which type of cooling to choose for an engine would not arise if the problems posed by air-cooled engines could readily be solved.

There are a number of excellent air-cooled commercial vehicle and industrial diesel engines, and they have also been successfully installed in boats although the disadvantage here is that the air ducts have to be so large that the designer has to integrate them from the start.

Obviously it would be a great advantage if it were possible to do without a water cooling circuit in a boat. Quite apart from that air-cooled engines are about 10–15% cheaper than water-cooled engines. As air-cooled engine speeds are 'governed' to a greater degree than water-cooled engines the power that the manufacturers extract is astonishing. The reason that these engines are not permitted to run faster, in other words, why they are governed, is because a great deal more cooling air would then be required.

Power output between the fuel tank and the speedometer
The next pages attempt to give as complete a picture as possible of what occurs between the fuel tank and the speedometer, using as little mathematics as possible.

On balance it is a sorry picture. While we have to accept the poor efficiency of the engine as a converter of energy, at least in terms of size, an owner should pay more attention to the propeller whose efficiency will decide whether, of the 30% of the fuel's energy that remains to be delivered to the shaft, again only 30–40% will be converted into thrust. The result would be that the efficiency of the whole installation would amount to a mere 10–15% whereas a figure of 25% should be the aim. This can only be achieved with high propeller efficiency of about 70%.

boat engines

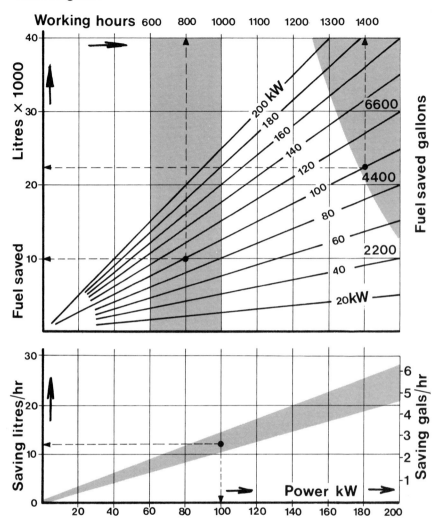

This graph shows how much less fuel is used by a diesel engine than a petrol engine, and is based solely on working hours related to engine power with no allowance made for the difference in cost of petrol and diesel oil. The vertical grey area shows the range of working hours where the higher purchase price of the diesel engine is paid off purely by lower consumption. The grey area top right shows roughly the number of engine hours at which the entire purchase price of the engine would be saved when compared with a similar petrol engine. Example: A 100 kW diesel uses about 10,000 litres (2,200 gallons) less fuel in about 800 working hours and that is roughly equivalent to the difference in purchase price. 800 hours is about 4–6 years use in a motor-sailer. If the 100 kW engine runs for 1,400 hours it will use about 22,000 litres (4,840 gallons) less fuel and this approximates to its purchase price.

Diesels cost about 20–40% more than petrol engines and the question is, when will this extra price be paid off due to the diesel's lower specific fuel consumption. The diagram shows the fuel saving by comparison with the petrol engine in litres and gallons per hour, and is related to differing power outputs so that you can see the figures for your engine at a glance. For example the 100 kW engine uses about 12·5 litres (2·75 gallons) less per hour than a 100 kW petrol engine.

The values shown here are mean values for marine engines given by several leading engine manufacturers.

	Petrol	Diesel
Length of service life	60–70%	100%
Repair costs		
500 hours	15%	4%
1,000 hours	76%	22%
1,500 hours	142%	100%

Comparing the durability and repair costs of petrol and diesel engines.

Country	Taxed diesel oil	Taxed normal petrol	Normal petrol % more expensive than diesel oil	Untaxed diesel oil	Untaxed petrol	Normal petrol % more expensive than diesel oil	% tax on diesel oil	% tax on normal petrol
B	61	96	36	35	40	12	43	58
DK	43	104	58	36	44	18	16	58
D	89	88	−0	39	35	−11	56	60
F	64	100	36	32	39	18	50	61
GB	68	69	−0	36	35	−3	47	49
I	41	94	56	30	36	16	27	62
NL	53	100	47	33	40	17	38	60
N	43	101	57	36	42	16	16	58
S	37	90	59	35	44	20	5	51

Comparison of fuel prices in European countries bordering on the sea.

boat engines

	Deutz F8L 413	Perkins TV 8.510 cc	Deutz BF8L 413	Volvo TAMD 70C
Cooling system	A	W	A	W
Rating B, British hp	214·6	229·3	268·2	265·5
Rev/min	2,650	2,600	2,650	2,500
No. and arrangement of cyls	8 V	8 V	8 V	6 L
Bore, ins	4·72	4·25	4·72	4·13
Stroke, ins	4·92	4·49	4·92	5·12
Swept volume, cu ins	689	510	689	411
Stroke to bore ratio	1·04	1·05	1·04	1·24
Mean piston speed ft/min	2,173	1,946	2,173	2,133
Specific power output				
Weight, lbs	1,764	2,094	1,984	1,918
Power to weight ratio lb/hp (British)	8·2	9·1	7·4	7·2
Length, ins	47·05	39·21	47·6	49·61
Breadth, ins	40·24	34·49	41·73	27·56
Height, ins	35·47	35·43	40·35	36·3
Volume, cu ft	38·86	27·73	46·38	28·72

Comparison of air-cooled and water-cooled diesel engines.
Above: data relating to one water-cooled and one air-cooled diesel engine of comparable output are listed side by side in five separate columns. Various calculated figures are included in addition to the normal specification values. The table is set out so that details of two comparable engines lie within two vertical lines. Where the measurement or characteristic of one engine is preferable to that of the other the value is blocked in grey, i.e. greater output and specific power output, smaller size, lower engine speed, mean piston speed and power to weight ratio. The small differences in the figures can be ignored if so desired because the grey area between two lines shows whether the advantage lies with the air-cooled or water-cooled engine. But first a few comments.

The weight figures have had to be adapted but, in my opinion, are adequate for comparisons to be made. The weights given for water-cooled engines are those of marine engines including heat exchanger and water-cooled exhaust as well as ancillaries, but without gears. I have added 20—50 kgs to the dry weights of the air-cooled engines without ancillaries as an alternative to subtracting some kilos from the fully-equipped boat engine weights.

NOTE: Swept volume—bore^2 × pi × no of cyls × stroke divided by 4:
Volume L × H × B divided by 12 × 12 × 12
Mean piston speed—stroke × 2 × rev/min divided by 12

Deutz BF6L 913	WM 130 T (Mercedes)	Hatz Z 108	VW 068.2	Hatz Z 788	Yanmar 2 QM	Conversion factor
A	W	A	W	A	W	
158·2	154·2	35·4	40·2	21·5	21·6	kW × 1·341022
2,800	2,800	3,000	3,600	3,000	2,900	No change
6 L	6 L	2 L	4 L	2 L	2 L	No change
4·02	3·82	4·25	2·99	3·54	3·46	mm × 0·1393701
4·92	5·04	4·33	3·15	3·54	3·54	mm × 0·0393701
375	347	123	88	70	67	Calculated
1·22	1·32	1·02	1·05	1·0	1·02	No change
2,296	2,352	2,165	1,890	1,770	1,711	Calculated
1,168	1,102	507	441	397	419	kg × 2·20462
7·4	7·1	14·3	11	18·5	19·4	Calculated
44·21	38·19	22·4	20·47	18·15	27·17	mm × 0·0393701
27·91	27·76	19·69	26·38	17·24	19·72	mm × 0·0393701
36·26	36·61	29·13	24·41	25·87	26·57	mm × 0·0393701
25·89	22·46	7·44	7·63	4·68	8·24	Calculated

The VW 068.2/M power output has been greatly reduced to make it comparable to the Hatz. A two-cylinder marine engine, of a real marine type, could of course be substituted for the very modern four-cylinder automobile engine, and the advantage would then lie very clearly with the air-cooled engine in this section.

The measurements for the air-cooled engines are without gearbox, and those of the water-cooled engines have been adjusted to match.

This table merely compares the actual engine values and ignores the problems of installation. Water-cooled engines are clearly preferable in this respect, and only in the power range below 20 kW do the figures favour air-cooled engines.

To go through the calculated values: the specific power output of the water-cooled engine is higher throughout; weight, and the power to weight ratio are inconclusive and it would be advisable to consider each unit separately. The power to weight ratio should be the more important factor when making a choice. The ratio is actually weight to power, the weight of the engine being divided by power output.

The measurements, and particularly the volume of water-cooled engines are much preferable, just as is the very much greater specific power output. Only the lower output air-cooled engines are smaller in size.

Conversions: m/s to ft/min = 196·8504. kg/kW to lb/Br.hp = 1·6439849. cu metre to cu ft = 35·31473. cu dm to cu in = 61·02399

23

boat engines

Power output and efficiency

Power output is a measure familiar to all those concerned with engines, but comparing the stated power outputs of even two engines is not easy. When it comes to such a fundamental matter as choosing an engine it is necessary to search more deeply to find the differences between them.

The amount of fuel delivered to the cylinder is controlled so that most of it is burnt when mixed with the air in the combustion chamber. Heat resulting from combustion increases pressure in the cylinder and this acts on the piston crown, thrusting the piston towards the crankshaft. This direct movement makes the crankshaft rotate because the connecting rod is attached eccentrically to the crankshaft.

The starting point is the energy (work) supplied by the fuel. What is measured at the shaft is the useful output or brake power of the engine. The ratio of brake power to fuel energy gives the figure for brake thermal efficiency.

This arises from the fundamental principle that Heat=Work. Heat (work) is measured in Joules. Fuel energy is measured in Joules per kilogramme, the fuel's calorific value being multiplied by the mass of fuel in kg. Work (J) is defined as Force (N) × Distance (m) while Power, the rate at which work is done, is measured in Watts (the rate of doing work at 1 Joule per second). In other words:

$$\text{Heat} \quad = \text{Energy (work)}$$
$$1 \text{ J} \quad = 1 \text{ Nm}$$
$$1 \text{ Joule} = 1 \text{ Newtonmetre}$$

$$\text{Power} = \text{Rate of work} \qquad = \text{Heat related to time}$$
$$1 \text{ W} \quad = 1 \text{ Nm/s} \qquad\qquad = 1 \text{ J/s}$$
$$1 \text{ Watt} = 1 \text{ Newtonmetre per sec} = 1 \text{ Joule per sec}$$

Thus the amount of heat introduced by the fuel, related to units of time, can be described as fuel power, and fuel power equals brake power measured on the test bench divided by brake thermal efficiency. Equally:

$$\text{Brake thermal efficiency} = \frac{\text{brake power}}{\text{fuel power}}$$

The energy balance:

The engine converts energy but great losses occur. Of the energy stored in the tank as fuel only about one third survives at the drive shaft; the rest is lost to friction etc, to the coolant and to the exhaust.

This 'effective' or useful third is then converted into boat speed by the propeller, again with significant losses which are discussed under the heading Propeller efficiency.

The speedometer indicates the real effectiveness of the installed unit but anyone interested needs first to consider various points which are discussed in the following pages.

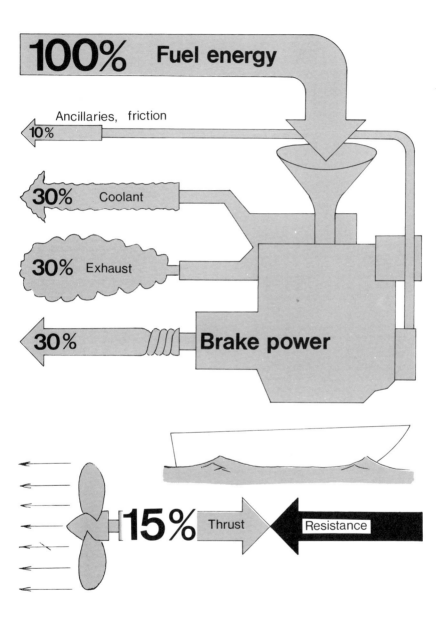

boat engines

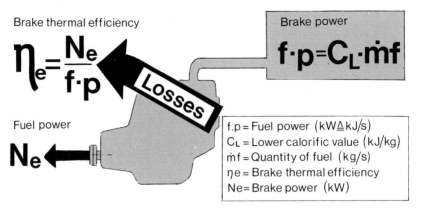

Brake thermal efficiency

$$\eta_e = \frac{Ne}{f \cdot p}$$

Brake power

$$f \cdot p = C_L \cdot \dot{m}f$$

Fuel power

$$Ne \longleftarrow$$

f.p = Fuel power $(kW \triangleq kJ/s)$
C_L = Lower calorific value (kJ/kg)
$\dot{m}f$ = Quantity of fuel (kg/s)
ηe = Brake thermal efficiency
Ne = Brake power (kW)

The sketch above shows the relationship between brake thermal efficiency and power output. As in technical publications the Greek letter eta, ' η ' is used here to denote efficiency. The subscript 'e' denotes effective or brake.

Opposite, top left
When the area beneath the curves in the indicator diagram opposite is converted into a rectangle the height of the rectangle gives the value for indicated mean effective pressure (P_i, imep). Brake mean effective pressure (bmep) can also be found in this way but will be smaller than imep due to mechanical losses. Bmep works on the piston crown as force F, the distance being the stroke (force × distance = work done). (Opposite, top right.)

Lower part of sketch opposite
The work done is converted into a turning moment on the crankshaft and is measured in brake tests as brake power when related to units of time.
    This is how the power formula is built up. If the individual elements are altered and considered their functions and interrelationships will easily be understood (see also Engine data).

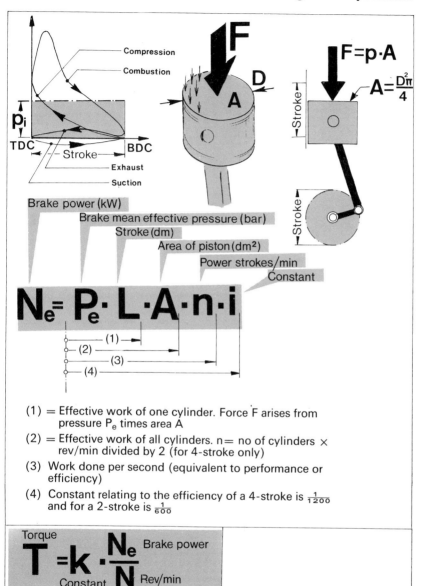

Compression

Combustion

p_i

TDC — Stroke — BDC

Exhaust

Suction

F

D — A

$F = p \cdot A$

$A = \dfrac{D^2 \pi}{4}$

Stroke

Stroke

Brake power (kW)
Brake mean effective pressure (bar)
Stroke (dm)
Area of piston (dm²)
Power strokes/min
Constant

$$N_e = P_e \cdot L \cdot A \cdot n \cdot i$$

——— (1) ——
— (2) ————————
——— (3) ————————
— (4) ————————————

(1) = Effective work of one cylinder. Force F arises from pressure P_e times area A

(2) = Effective work of all cylinders. n= no of cylinders × rev/min divided by 2 (for 4-stroke only)

(3) Work done per second (equivalent to performance or efficiency)

(4) Constant relating to the efficiency of a 4-stroke is $\frac{1}{1200}$ and for a 2-stroke is $\frac{1}{600}$

Torque

$$T = k \cdot \dfrac{N_e}{N}$$

Brake power

Constant   Rev/min

boat engines

Fuel power is simply the energy supplied by the fuel per second multiplied by the calorific value of the fuel.

The ratio of brake thermal efficiency to indicated thermal efficiency equals the mechanical efficiency of the engine, and mechanical efficiency is a measure of the drop in power resulting from mechanical losses, including power extracted to drive ancillary equipment such as pumps.

In practice thermal efficiency is required as well as brake thermal efficiency and

$$\text{Indicated thermal efficiency} = \frac{\text{indicated power}}{\text{fuel power}}$$

Indicated power is the power developed in the cylinders and is a measure of the work done on the piston by the gases in the cylinder. Mechanical efficiency is also the ratio of brake power measured at the output shaft to indicated power.

In the case of a high speed engine indicated power can only be measured electronically with an oscillograph, and this is not generally available. The recording oscillometer measures and draws the changes in pressure during a complete cycle, thus producing an indicator diagram (see right). This can be produced mechanically for slow running engines, but these are not used in yachts. This leaves only one way to compare the brake thermal efficiency of different engines and for this an exact definition is required of the rating and other stated values. The indicated power can be calculated from the area of the indicator diagram. The next step is to find a figure, purely by calculation, for mean pressure which is one of the most important characteristics of an engine.

If you imagine the relatively complicated area of an indicator diagram as a rectangle of similar area, the height of this rectangle represents the indicated mean effective pressure inside the cylinder during a complete cycle. This pressure would do the same amount of work as is actually obtained during one cycle. This leads on to a power output formula which is made up of the most vital engine statistics. The formula can start with brake power if brake mean effective pressure is to be included, and this is a figure frequently found in good leaflets giving engine details. (The formula is used to determine the design of an engine and, alternatively, can be used for purposes of comparison engine data and figures for making comparisons.)

Propeller

Far too little attention is paid to the propeller, and above all to its efficiency. For instance, with a typical choice of propeller diameter today, 30% of the fuel energy remaining at the propeller shaft can be halved again and propeller efficiency still be considered good! Everything written about propellers is set out by designers for designers, and the engine owner finds that the mathematics involved are beyond him. In consequence we use propellers too small in diameter and very poor efficiency is the result.

Even if the nominal output of an engine is known, mechanical efficiency at the propeller estimated, and boat speed measured it is impossible to estimate the propeller's efficiency with any certainty although conclusions can be formed on hull design and the actual power delivered by the engine installation. Nor am I

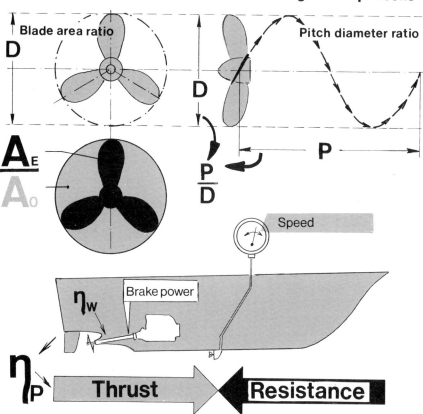

The nominal rating is stated on the engine itself; mechanical losses up to the propeller can be estimated fairly accurately (e.g. mechanical efficiency η_m for one bearing and the stuffing box $= 0\cdot80$); boat speed can be calculated over a measured distance or noted on the speedometer (do they agree?); the propeller measurements are known (diameter, pitch, number of blades, blade-area ratio). What is not known at first, and what would be of the greatest interest, is thrust or resistance. Other data must be used if reliable conclusions are to be drawn on the engine installation and the boat. In many cases the propeller manufacturer states a value for propeller efficiency, but unless this has actually come from and is guaranteed by the propeller manufacturer himself the value must be used with caution. You will see on the next pages how high these values can be.

boat engines

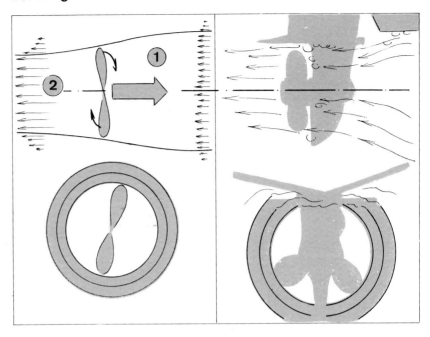

The sketches illustrate the momentum theory of the screw, much simplified, and show how the propeller exerts thrust, regardless of the shape of the blade sections and the thickness or number of blades. The propeller, the component responsible for propulsion, converts engine torque (work) into thrust or advance (work). As the propeller rotates it draws in water (1), accelerates it in the disc area around the propeller, and dispatches it aft at a correspondingly greater speed (2). Thrust is generated by the acceleration of the water, and the amount of water accelerated depends both on the advance velocity of the propeller (boat speed) and the disc diameter (propeller diameter). Thrust multiplied by boat speed equals the useful power developed by a propeller. It is not merely complicated but impracticable to use this theory to make even approximately accurate calculations because the turbulence caused by propeller shaft brackets, the shaft itself, and disturbance to the flow beneath the hull cannot be worked out mathematically. This is the reason why the results of propeller research based on tests of models are used in practice.

Propeller efficiency follows on from this theory, and conclusions can be drawn as to what degree of efficiency can actually be achieved. The formula looks rather complicated, but is quite simple if a pocket calculator is used.

$$B_{P1} = \frac{N \times \sqrt{P}}{V_A^2 \times \sqrt{V_A}} = N \times \sqrt{\frac{P}{V_A^5}}$$

30

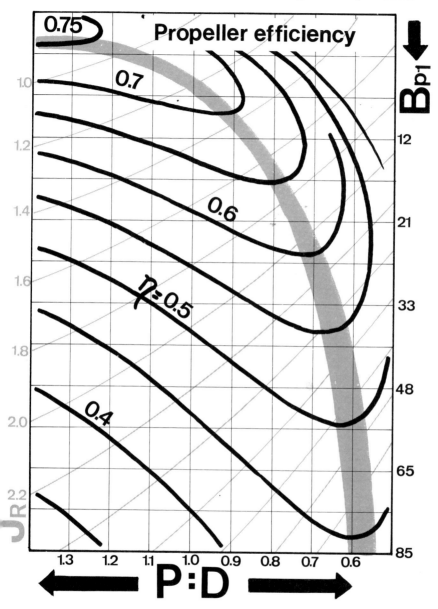

Propeller efficiency

boat engines

V_A is the advance velocity of the propeller and

$$V_A = V_S \times (1 - W)$$

The abbreviations used here accord with those used in the Wageningen experiments:

N = propeller rotative speed, rev/min
P = power in SHP, Shaft Horse Power
V_A = advance velocity in knots
V_S = boat speed in knots
W = wake fraction, as % of V_S (for values see p. 33)
f = propeller rotative speed, rev/sec
D = propeller diameter in feet

The diagram on page 31 is a simplified version of the Wageningen diagram for determining optimum propeller diameter. The values relate to a three-bladed propeller with a blade-area ratio of 0·5 (Wageningen B 3–50).

The scale on the right gives the power loading coefficient B_{P1} (C_P is also used sometimes), calculated from shaft horse power, rotative propeller speed and advance velocity as above.

The figures on the left hand scale, J_R, are the reciprocal values of the advance coefficient, J, and are therefore equal to diameter multiplied by propeller revolutions per second, divided by advance velocity.

$$J_R = \frac{1}{J} = \frac{f \times D}{V_A}$$

To find the efficiency of a particular propeller, use the pitch to diameter ratio on the horizontal scale and the relevant J_R (see example A below). When calculating measurements which will result in a high degree of efficiency, stay within the grey area which indicates maximum efficiency to find the optimum diameter (see example B).

Example A: how efficient is a given propeller? The pitch to diameter ratio is known, and this fixes the vertical coordinate. J_R can be calculated from advance velocity, propeller diameter and the rotative propeller speed (f). Efficiency is read off the graph where the two lines intersect, and can be checked against the power loading coefficient B_{P1}.

Example B: determining optimum propeller measurements. This time it is a question of gradually working towards the shaded area from the power loading coefficient B_{P1} and from the reciprocal of the advance coefficient J_R. Shaft horse power is known and advance velocity calculated, but propeller diameter and propeller rotative speeds (f and N) must be varied, the aim being to use the greatest possible diameter and the lowest possible rotative speed. Low rotative speed is achieved by reducing engine revolutions to the minimum with reduction gear. Naturally there is a limit to the propeller diameter possible, and this has to be taken into account, as does the fact that, at faster speeds, higher rotative speed increases efficiency.

The aim should be as follows, or higher:

engine comparisons

Sailing boats with auxiliary engines   0·40
Displacement boats (motor-sailers, motor cruisers)   0·60
Semi-displacement boats   0·65–0·70
Planing boats   0·70
Extremely light planing boats and racing boats   up to 0·80

Wake fraction
Turbulence leads, among other things, to a difference between boat speed and advance velocity, and this is called the wake fraction. The following allowances should be made:

Displacement boats, long keel, heavy, slow   20–25%
Displacement boats, narrow, relatively light   20–15%
Semi-displacement boats   15–10%
Planing cruisers   10–5%
Light planing boats   7–3%
Racing boats   3%

The reduction ratios generally employed nowadays for different types of boats at appropriate engine speeds are shown below (always aim to the right). The horizontal scale gives the speed to length ratio (V√/WL), and the types of propeller suitable for the various ratios are drawn above. 1 = folding propeller

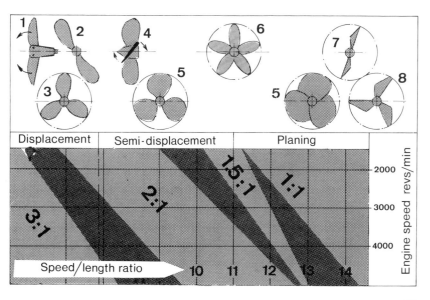

33

boat engines

for sailing boats; low propeller efficiency, but very little resistance when the boat is under sail. 2 = fixed two-bladed propeller which continues to turn when the boat is under sail. 3 = normal three-bladed propeller for a displacement boat, used up to planing boat range. 4 = controllable pitch propeller, used almost exclusively with lower power units in sailing boats. The blades are feathered in the sailing position so that little resistance is offered, and no reverse gear is required. Efficiency is poor and the mechanism is generally very vulnerable to sand and impurities. 5 = three-bladed propeller; for boats with a high speed-length ratio the blade-area ratio is increased to over 1:1. 6 = four- and five-bladed propellers in general use in larger yachts give very high efficiency and quiet running. 7 = speed propeller for extremely light sporting and racing boats. 8 = for light, fast sporting boats.

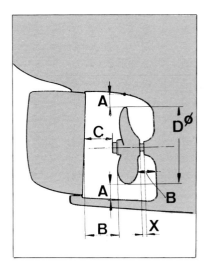

The shape of the hull dictates the maximum propeller diameter. A displacement boat is shown in the sketch, but this is equally true of a planing boat. A is the most important measurement. To avoid noise and unpleasant vibration the gap between the propeller tips and the hull should be at least 50 mm or 10% of the diameter D. C should be 120 mm more than the propeller boss fittings to avoid unshipping the rudder when the propeller is changed. About 10 mm clearance is allowed at X.

The upper half of a propeller works in lower water pressure than does the lower half. Furthermore the blades work in turbulence caused by the shaft brackets or keel, and this causes vibration. To counter this effect an irregular number of blades is used (three instead of two) so that only one blade vibrates as it passes through the turbulent area rather than the whole propeller. An alternative is to shape the blade like a sickle. The result is quieter running. The

34

difference in pressure between the upper and lower part also causes sideways thrust which forces the stern to the right when the propeller is right-handed or to the left when it is left-handed. When the boat is motoring astern the opposite occurs and the boat is pushed towards the other side (left-handed to the right, right-handed to the left). This effect is barely noticeable when running ahead, but is very evident when in astern gear or manoeuvring, and many owners consequently have a 'good' and 'bad' side when coming alongside, depending on which way the propeller rotates. If the hull has been badly designed the effect can be so marked that this sideways thrust cannot be countered in spite of putting the helm hard over.

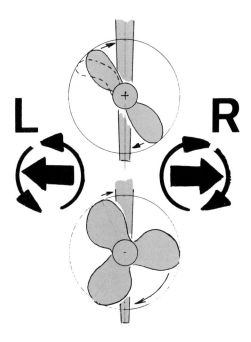

Damage and repairs to the propeller.
Sketch A: small dents and roughness can be smoothed with a file, but be careful not to unbalance the propeller by working on one blade only. If there is pitting at the root of the blade (arrowed) your propeller is suffering from cavitation (due to formation of local cavities in the water). This can be caused by too high a rotational speed, the wrong propeller (blade-area ratio) or a poorly designed hull. Ask an expert.
Sketch B: badly bent or broken blades can be repaired, but only by a specialist repair shop. Use a spare propeller in the meantime.

boat engines

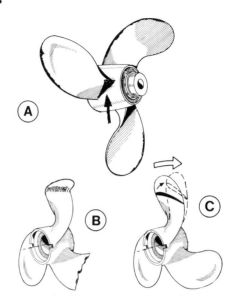

Sketch C: It is very difficult to detect a slight bend in a blade visually but the damage makes itself felt through noisy operation and a reduction in speed (repair shop). Warning: Every time the propeller strikes an object keep a check on the gearbox oil level, listen to be sure that the engine is not running more noisily and watch for leaks at the stern tube (if you have an outdrive do not confuse this with oil from the exhaust).

Be careful to put the gear into neutral when changing the propeller. If the engine is warm there is a danger that it could start immediately you turn the propeller and you could then lose a finger. To loosen the propeller nut jam a piece of wood (keep one in your tool box) between the propeller and the cavitation plate. Depending on the type of engine you must either switch off the ignition, remove the ignition safety fuse, disconnect the plugs or operate the stop control.

able to give you a magic formula which will tell you at a glance how efficient your propeller is. However, with a little patience and a pocket calculator you should be able to follow me.

There has been considerable research into propeller development (Schaffran in Germany, Gawn in England, Taylor in the USA) while latterly very intensive research has been carried out in the Dutch test tank in Wageningen (Wageningen B-Screw series). I have used the latter as a basis for determining propeller efficiency as set out in the following pages. But first let us consider the situation as it exists for the purchaser or owner. As in the figure (page 33) you have, or are able to obtain, figures giving:

the engine's rating
estimated mechanical efficiency, engine to propeller
propeller measurements (diameter, pitch, area of the blades)
propeller revolutions and
boat speed.

One figure is not known, the value for propeller efficiency which would indicate how much power the propeller actually uses to overcome resistance.

The propeller measurements, pitch and diameter, are given in mm or inches depending on the manufacturer. The blade-area ratio is provided occasionally, and this indicates the ratio of the area of the blade surfaces to the full disc area swept by the blades. The number of blades is evident. Efficiency should be taken as guaranteed at the appropriate engine speed.

The difference between ideal screw efficiency, which is the product of pitch x propeller revolutions, and the actual advance of the boat is slip. Many people are tempted into trying to use slip to establish efficiency, but unfortunately this is wrong because many other factors are involved when calculating slip. Equally false is the assumption that an optimum propeller has little slip, or even that ideal screw efficiency could be achieved.

It is far better to imagine the propeller sucking in water like a pump, accelerating it and then thrusting it aft. This is shown in the sketch on p. 30 which is a simplified version of the momentum theory of the screw. The function and relationship between the different values can be far better grasped with this in mind, and the diagram on p. 31 showing how to determine the efficiency of a propeller will be better understood.

Pages 29 ff. show individual points that are important in practice. The speed-propeller-engine relationship will be further discussed in the chapter headed 'Correct handling'.

Fuel consumption

Heat is generated by fuel combustion and heat, as has already been explained, is equivalent to work (similar units).

In other words, when you ship a tankful of fuel you are loading work which will later be released by combustion.

The quantity of fuel consumed by an engine depends partly on the power of the engine and partly on how efficiently it is used.

A certain quantity of fuel, for example one kilogramme, has a certain calorific value which is measured in units of Joules per kilogramme. As the composition of fuel varies slightly the lower calorific value (C_L) is used, and this indicates the minimum calorific value to be extracted from a kilogramme of fuel.

$$\text{Quantity of fuel (kg)} \times \text{Calorific value (J/kg)} = \text{Amount of heat (J)}$$
$$\text{Fuel} \quad \times \quad C_L \quad = \quad Q \text{ (J)}$$

Arising from this, and from the relationships already given

$$\text{Work (Nm)} = \text{Heat (J)} = \text{Amount of fuel (kg)} \times \text{Calorific value (J/kg)}$$

When the quantity of fuel used for work is related to another factor, in this case time, a new performance characteristic is obtained, fuel consumption or, to

boat engines

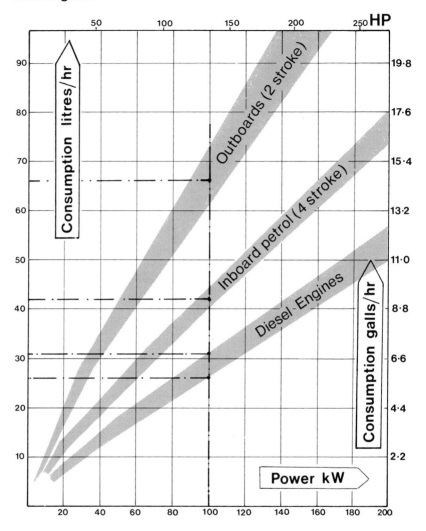

Hourly fuel consumption in litres and gallons for outboards (two-stroke petrol engines), for inboard petrol engines (four-stroke) and for diesel engines (four-stroke). Direct injection diesels lie at the bottom of the consumption area shown, and indirect injection diesels at the top edge. The graph is based on averages between rated speed and minimum specific fuel consumption at maximum torque. The example entered shows the consumption of a 100 kW engine:

Diesel (direct)	26 litres/hr	215 g/kWh	5·7 gals/hr
Diesel (indirect)	31 litres/hr	260 g/kWh	6·82 gals/hr
Petrol (four-stroke)	42 litres/hr	305 g/kWh	9·24 gals/hr
Petrol (two-stroke)	67 litres/hr	490 g/kWh	14·7 gals/hr

be correct, hourly fuel consumption.

For example: you are sailing from Plymouth to X and use 17·6 gallons (80 litres) of diesel oil. Little can be established from this fact, and very little more if you know that the distance is about 54 miles (87 km). However, if you add that you have sailed from Plymouth to X and that your hourly fuel consumption was 4·4 gals (20 litres) you can establish that the time taken was four hours and that your speed was $13\frac{1}{2}$ knots (25 km/hr).

If you have read this far carefully you will have noticed already that, when considering formulae, fuel is measured in kilogrammes but as soon as the boat enters the picture it is measured in gallons or litres. Technical calculations are made in kg because the figures are easier to work with, whereas the quantity the skipper ships on board is measured in gallons. Sailors therefore also talk in terms of gallons, just as solid fuel is bought in tons.

You will often need to use the following conversion factors:
Density is measured in kg/dm^3 which is the same as kg/litre.

Diesel oil	0·81–0·84 kg/dm^3
Normal petrol	0·72–0·74 kg/dm^3
Super petrol	0·75–0·78 kg/dm^3

One litre of diesel oil weighs between 0·82 and 0·84 kg (one gallon between 3·73 and 3·82 kg) but for calculations we shall use

Diesel oil: 1 litre=0·83 kg=830 g: 1 gallon=3·77 kg=377 g
Normal petrol: 1 litre=0·73 kg=730 g: 1 gallon=3·32 kg=332 g
Super petrol: 1 litre=0·76 kg=760 g: 1 gallon=3·45 kg=345 g

And when converting kilogrammes to litres and gallons

Diesel oil: 1 kg=1·21 litres 1 kg=·2662 gallons
Normal petrol: 1 kg=1·37 litres 1 kg=·3014 gallons
Super petrol: 1 kg=1·32 litres 1 kg=·2904 gallons

As was made clear in the example above, virtually no information can be gleaned purely from the quantity of petrol used, but the distance covered can be determined when total consumption and hourly consumption are known. The next step relates hourly fuel consumption to engine power and gives the value for specific fuel consumption which is measured in grammes per kilowatt and hour.

Specific fuel consumption is an important feature when comparing and evaluating engines. The manufacturer declares fuel consumption at full load in grammes per kilowatt hour, but it is only when fuel consumption is related to units of power that an exact comparison between a number of engines can be made. As a rough guide:

boat engines

Diesel oil—1 litre or ·22 gals every 3 kW hours
Petrol   —1 litre every 2 kW hours

So if your engine salesman tells you that a certain 40 kW diesel engine only uses 10 litres an hour you should suspect that he is not very knowledgeable and that, probably, an expert has told him that, when installed in the boat, the engine will use 10 litres per hour at 80% of its rated speed (see also paragraph relating to partial load curve on p. 68).

Further information on consumption will be found in the chapter 'Handling the engine properly'.

The table below shows that the combustion method and the power range or size of the engine are decisive when it comes to specific fuel consumption. The table on p. 41 also shows how consumption varies but in relation to load and engine speed.

Type of engine	Power (kW)	Specific fuel consumption		
		g/kWh	g/hp-hr(Br)	litres/kWh
Petrol (2-stroke)	1–100	over 380	over 280	over 0·52
Petrol (4-stroke)	1–300	380–270	280–200	0·52–0·37
Diesel (4-stroke, direct)	50–100	260–240	190–180	0·31–0·29
Diesel (4-stroke, indirect)	50–100	300–280	220–210	0·36–0·34
Diesel (4-stroke)	1–300	300–220	220–160	0·36–0·27
Diesel (4-stroke)	300–2,000	240–220	180–160	0·29–0·27
Diesel (4-stroke)	2,000–15,000	230–210	170–160	0·28–0·25
Diesel (2-stroke)	5,000–35,000	220–210	160–160	0·27–0·25
Rotary engine	50–100	410–300	310–220	0·50–0·36
Gas turbine engine	50–2,000	1,100–340	820–250	1·33–0·41

The differences between the values are less important for evaluation, however, because the power range will already be known and it is extremely unlikely that there will be any doubt over which combustion method to choose.

The differences, then, are either a few grammes per kilowatt hour or small changes in the course of the consumption curve, and it is essential to have an exact definition of the standard test conditions under which the figures were obtained. In other words, it is impossible to compare engine A's fuel consumption related to overloadable continuous rating A with figures for engine B based on a commercial vehicle rating in accordance with DIN 70020 (see Comparing power output).

How vitally important this is can be appreciated by comparing the consumption of a direct injection 100 kW diesel engine; this is shown on p. 38 as 215 g/kWh, above as 260–240 g/kWh and on p. 19 as 300–220 g/kWh. All these figures are correct; it is only the definition that differs.

The table shows that the tendency is for the specific fuel consumption of

engine comparisons

smaller engines to be greater than that of larger engines. Values such as these are, of course, best suited to making comparisons, and can be very useful as a rough guide, for example when discussing consumption during a purchase.

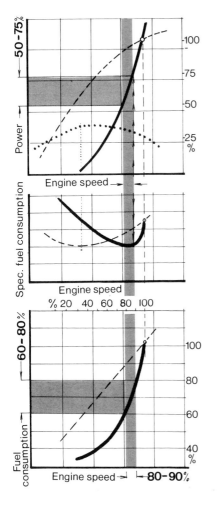

Specific fuel consumption and hourly fuel consumption related to full load (broken line) and to partial load or the power absorbed by the propeller (solid line).

Top: The torque curve at full load is shown dotted below the power curves and is included to emphasize the fact that specific fuel consumption is lowest when torque is highest (best combustion, highest brake mean effective pressure).

Centre: The specific fuel consumption curve as engine speed increases. The best consumption figures are under partial load at about 80–90% of rated speed, in the 50–75% power output range, but values rise steeply far above the full load figures as engine speed decreases (see performance graph on p. 76).

Lower: Hourly fuel consumption when power absorption by the propeller matches partial load shows clearly that, when engine speed is reduced by 10–20%, hourly consumption drops to almost half that at full load (rated speed). Remember this and use the engine speed control sensitively because this is the only way to achieve economy (see also Range).

41

boat engines

Comparing power output

An exact definition of the conditions under which the engine has been bench tested is essential if power figures given for different engines are to be compared. Standards have been set up so that comparisons between manufacturers' figures can be as realistic as possible. Unfortunately international agreement has not been universal as yet and, consequently, it may be a question of dealing both with differing standard test conditions and with either maximum or continuous output.

First, however, we must consider the unit used for power. The internationally agreed SI system does not use horse power as a unit. To anyone who has used horse power for a life time the use of the new kilowatt as the unit for power seems an abstract idea because formerly it was used only in connection with electricity. When you settle your electricity account you pay so much per kWhr and this certainly sounds more familiar. You check the number of units on your meter or, to put it more precisely, you read how much power in kW has passed through the meter, and this is multiplied by the appropriate time in hours. You therefore pay for the work you have taken from the electricity grid, work which the current has performed for you.

$$\text{Power (kW)} \times \text{Time (h)} = \text{Work (kWh) or Power (kW)} = \frac{\text{Work (kWh)}}{\text{Time (h)}}$$

It is easy enough to understand the kilowatt in relation to electricity. One kW of course = 1,000 watts. The first stage of a fan heater probably uses 1,000 watts and with the second stage uses 2,000 watts. To some extent this makes it possible to envisage how horse power was used for decades. One metric horse power was the unit for raising 75 kp one metre every second, while one British horse power was the unit for raising 1 lb 550 ft every second; thus it can be said that power (hp) is work (kp/m or ft-lbs) divided by units of time (seconds). This was the same formula as the kW formula. Let us look at them again:

Power (kW) = Work (kWh) : Time (h)
Power (hp) = Work (kpm or ft-lbs) : Time (s)

All that remains is to establish the relationship between the two:

1 kw = 1,000 watts = 1,000 Joules per second
1,000 Joules = 1,000 Nm = 102 kpm

Therefore 1 kw = 102/75 metric hp = 1·36 metric hp and
1 metric hp = 75/102 kW = ·736 kW
Similarly 1 kW = 1·34 British hp and 1 British hp = ·7457 kW
1 metric hp = ·9863 British hp and 1 British hp = 1·0139 metric hp.
So much for the relationship between kilowatts and horse power.

To return to comparing power outputs: if manufacturer A states that his engine has a rated output of 100 kW, the same figure as is given by manufacturer B, it does not mean that both engines are equally powerful, and yet neither manufacturer is lying.

It is only possible to compare the statement rated output = 100 kW if it is also stated exactly under what test conditions the power was measured. In other words, not only must the atmospheric conditions have been the same but it must be known whether the engine was tested with ancillary fittings, with

42

exhaust and air filter fitted as for normal use etc, or not. Another important point is whether the engine was overloadable at the rating given, and much more besides.

There are a number of standards in current use which unfortunately still differ, but they are to be amended to ISO (International Standardizing Organization) recommendations within the next few years. In Germany all measurements are based on DIN standards and this has led to the description DIN hp which logically should lead to DIN kW. The use of the prefix DIN does not guarantee that the unit of power is particularly reliable. This will only be the case when the standard to which the figure relates is also given. DIN ratings are used in a number of other European countries and are given by some British manufacturers. In Britain the current standard for diesel engines is BS AU 141a.

DIN 70020 is the standard for road vehicle engines. The output is measured at the flywheel with all normal ancillaries fitted. The effective power deviation allowed is ±5%. Atmospheric test conditions are laid down as:

Air pressure 1,013 millibars
Air temperature at the air intake 20°C

It is important to note that the tests are made with the air filter, fan, exhaust etc fitted as for normal use.

DIN 6270, the second standard, includes the data for determining the power of all commercial vehicle and industrial engines. Two ratings are used, depending on the type of duty to be performed by the engine.

● Continuous rating A, overload permissible, is the maximum effective output measured at the flywheel that the engine, depending on the type of duty, is capable of delivering over a long period; output is limited to permit an overload rating.

The overload rating mentioned in continuous rating A means that the engine can be overloaded. It is the maximum effective output that can be delivered continuously or intermittently for one hour out of twelve, and is generally about 10% higher than continuous rating A.

● Continuous rating B is the maximum effective output that can be developed by an engine for a definite period relevant to its application, and output is limited so that rating B is not exceeded. The limit is determined by the length of time that full rating B output is required, and this depends on the engine's application.

Rating B normally requires the engine to deliver rating B output continuously for one hour during a six hour period at varying speeds. This is not invariable and rating B can also relate to uninterrupted continuous use when it is classed as continuous rating B.

There is also a rating B for special applications. Output relevant to the intended application is declared by the manufacturer and no overload is permissible.

● Maximum output is the highest output that an engine can deliver for 15 minutes without mechanical or thermal overloading. It is of little importance and mainly serves to prove that the engine is working below its full capacity at rating B.

The following are some examples of engine applications relating to the two

boat engines

DIN 6270 definitions. For example continuous rating A, overload permissible, relates to:
Engines used for marine propulsion, especially ocean-going vessels
Stationary electricity generating machinery operating continuously
Engines for pumps or other machinery with constant load and continuous operation
Drilling, power for the drill
Rating B relates to:
Engines for machinery for industrial appliances where the load changes markedly
Road construction plant
Drilling, winch drive
Propulsion for special vessels, such as police and rescue launches, patrol boats etc.
Pleasure craft and yachts, or rather their engine ratings, fall into the rating B group, but a distinction is often made and rating B for special applications applies.

Power is measured at the flywheel and is the effective output delivered by the engine when the ancillary fittings needed to operate the engine, according to its application, (such as ignition, injection pump, scavenging and cooling blowers, water pump, radiator fan, compressor etc.) are being driven by the engine.
The atmospheric conditions at the time of testing are laid down as:
Air pressure 981 millibars or 736 mm Hg
Air temperature at air intake 20°C
Relative humidity 60%

Unlike road engine rating DIN 70020, DIN 6270 permits no deviation. Because power output always varies slightly (the figure of $\pm5\%$ of nominal output is usual today) figures consequently have to be on the low side to comply with DIN 6270.
BS AU 141a takes account of ISO recommendations and relates to diesel engines with a wide range of duties. Power output is presented in the form of performance curves showing maximum brake power at various speeds. Gross brake output is measured with only those auxiliaries essential to the engine's operation being directly driven. Engine speed is specified by the manufacturer. Installed brake power output, on the other hand, is that delivered when all the equipment required for a particular vehicle installation is fitted.
Standard test conditions are: air pressure 101·5 kN/m² 760 mm Hg, air temperature at inlet 20°C: humidity is neglected.
Between the initial and final test presented as curves there is a 100 hour test run in 10 separate periods with at least two hours gap between each of them. Each period consists of five cycles, and each cycle includes three-quarter load at maximum declared speed, full load at a speed matching maximum torque, idling, and full load at maximum speed. Exhaust opacity is also measured.

Other standards
● Society of Automotive Engineers (SAE). Warning: it used to be taken generally that SAE tests resulted in 20% higher figures because the engines

44

were tested without ancillaries, filter and exhaust. That is out of date! Net SAE output based on the current standard J816b is several per cent lower than that of road engines rated under DIN 70020 (Mercedes figures show about 8%). This is also why SAE horse power has disappeared from brochures lately; it is less effective for publicity purposes. Naturally if older pamphlets are referred to be careful to check whether the rating was obtained before or after the new standard.

● Commissione Unificazione Normalizzazione Autoveicoli, (CUNA) figures are about 5–10% higher than DIN 70020.

● Conseil International des Machines à Combustion (CIMAC). In 1961, as agreed by Austria, Belgium, Britain, Denmark, France, Germany, Italy, Japan, the Netherlands, Spain, Sweden, Switzerland and the USA, recommendations were published by CIMAC with a view to making international trade easier. DIN ratings accord with CIMAC recommendations.

You may pick up a German pamphlet and wish to make comparisons, so here are the German equivalents to the terms used:

Brake power or effective output	Nutzleistung
Continuous overloadable rating A	Dauerleistung A
Rating B	Leistung B
Overload rating	Überleistung
Maximum output	Höchstleistung
and in CIMAC recommendations:	
Continuous brake power	Dauerleistung A
Full stop brake power	Leistung B (blockiert)
Overload power	Überleistung

Standardization and progress continue, of course, and we are changing over to SI units. DIN 6270 will be replaced soon by DIN 6271, a standard with an even broader base internationally as it stems from ISO recommendations. This will be of particular interest to yacht owners because boat and ship engines will be more thoroughly dealt with by this standard (different test conditions etc.).

boat engines

Engine data and figures for making comparisons

Figures relating to performance characteristics enable technical aspects of engines to be compared, though they are essentially relative. If any real comparisons are to be made these figures must be related to a common standard, and this is not too easy to achieve from the information supplied by manufacturers. Furthermore, because very many interrelated factors affect the value given for a specific characteristic, it cannot be viewed in isolation. An uninformed reader might assume that the highest or lowest figure would be best, but this is by no means always the case due to their being interdependent; altering one causes others to alter too. In spite of this apparent disorder clear lines can be drawn. As an engine purchaser it is the finished product that is of concern and all that is required is to classify the details appropriately and to evaluate them.

The following example shows how these figures can be interpreted: you want an engine for your boat with an output of about 40 kW (54 hp). Six makes are on sale and vary in power from 36–45 kW (48–60 hp). Whereas fuel consumption in gallons or litres per hour will be important later at sea you need to know which engine delivers most power while consuming least fuel, and this information is given by the figure for specific fuel consumption. This gives the amount of fuel consumed in grammes or cubic centimetres per kilowatt hour. Comparing the figures below makes this clear:

Engine A: Power 36 kW: Fuel consumption 15 1/hr: 3·3 gals/hr;
Specific fuel consumption 350 g/kWh
Engine B: Power 45 kW: Fuel consumption 17 1/hr: 3·7 gals/hr
Specific fuel consumption 314 g/kWh

Although engine A uses two litres (·44 gals) less fuel per hour than engine B the latter consumes 36 grammes less fuel when delivering one kilowatt for one hour.

This shows which engine works more economically, and also shows how carefully such values must be considered. Here the difference is only 36 grammes, but suppose that you are thinking in terms of a 1,000 kW engine and one thousand hours use. The difference then amounts to over 40,000 litres or 40 tonnes (8,800 gals), enough to heat six houses in the winter.

Naturally there are a number of factors which have to be considered, and the emphasis varies from boat to boat. In a heavy displacement boat the lightness of the engine is relatively less important, and the choice of a 10 kW diesel engine for a sailing boat should not be based purely on specific fuel consumption. First decide which are the really vital factors, and then weigh up the engines.

It must be repeated that the buyer rarely has the opportunity to choose the engine to suit the boat when he purchases a series-produced boat. It is in individual cases that these factors really matter. Anyone interested in design or boatbuilding should pay particular attention to the following pages.

Arrangement of cylinders

With a given boat, and the transmission and the position of the engine already decided, it may well be that cylinder arrangement is the determining factor when a choice is made.

engine comparisons

Type	Cylinder No and arrangement	Rating B Rev/min	Length A in mm	Breadth B in mm	Height C in mm	Volume A × B × C in dm³
Deutz BF 6L 413	6 cyl vee	140/2,650	1,035 ng	1,060	1,002	1,099
Deutz F 6L 413R	6 cyl i-l	122/2,650	1,452 ng	755	1,012	1,109
Farymann S30	2 cyl vee	20–2,500	550 ng / 780 g	655	572	206 / 292
Bukh 20	2 cyl i-l	15/3,000	560 ng / 820 g	457	672	172 / 252
Yanmar 2 QM 20	2 cyl i-l	16/2,700	555 ng / 825 g	500	675	187 / 278
Marine Craft Ford 26 H	6 cyl vee	104/5,500	712 ng / 965 g	674	620	297 / 403
Volvo BB 170A	6 cyl i-l	104/5,000	960 ng / 1,392 g	570	660	361 / 523
MTU 8R	8 cyl i-l	630/1,600	2,730	1,120	1,840	5,626
MTU 16 V	16 cyl vee	1,260/1,600	3,100	1,650	1,870	9,565

The table compares the dimensions of in-line (L) and vee (V) engines. In the case of very small 15–20 kW diesels the difference in design only affects height because the shape would otherwise become distorted, especially with a gearbox fitted. The compactness of the vee engines is shown by comparing the volume of the two Deutz engines; this is almost the same although the vee engine output is higher. Similarly although the 16-cylinder MTU develops double the output of the 8-cylinder in-line MTU the volume is only 70% greater. The volume of the two petrol engines, the Ford and the Volvo, compared to those of the small diesels shows how much more power is extracted from petrol engines.

47

boat engines

The two most common cylinder arrangements are shown below, taking the two Deutz engines listed in the table (page 47) as an example. The main measurements which give the volume, A = length, B = breadth, C = height, show the main differences between the two designs.

In-line engine = long, narrow, tall
Vee engine   = short, wide, low

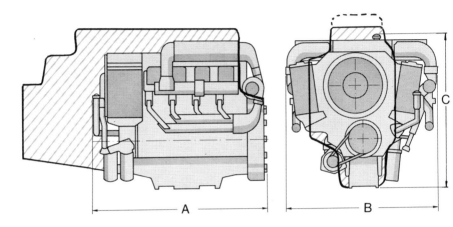

In-line engines are high and long but narrow. A variation is the horizontal engine which is long and wide, but low. The upper limit for a high-speed in-line engine is six cylinders (this is not true of low-speed ships' diesels, e.g. 16-cylinders in line).

Vee engines are lower and shorter than in-line engines. Although some problems arise they are in widespread use in commercial vehicles because they are so compact. The whole block is more squat which is advantageous both as to space and weight when compared with in-line engines.

Other arrangements are exceptional in the boat engine sector.

Petrol engines Apart from Ford who also produce a four-cylinder vee engine, petrol engines up to four cylinders are in-line engines. Almost all six-cylinder engines are vee engines, apart from Volvo's six-cylinder 118 kW engines which are in-line.

European eight cylinder engines have virtually died out (118 kW Porsche 928, 165 kW Mercedes 450 SLC) and only American eight-cylinder vee engines are still sold. This is true of the 170 kW Volvo too because this is an American engine marinized by Volvo.

Diesel engines In-line engines are general, with six or more cylinders as well because engine speeds are far lower than those of petrol engines, and because they are used in commercial vehicles for different purposes. Six-cylinder vee engines start at about 140 kW (petrol engines above about 70 kW). The only exception is Farymann who are already producing twin cylinder vee engines.

48

A six-cylinder in-line engine sold in either horizontal or vertical form is used here to show how one or other form will be more suitable depending on the space available. The measurements are:

Type	Design	Power	Rev/min	Length	Breadth	Height
Volvo THAM D 70	horizontal	198 kW	2,500	1,650	1,040	670
Volvo TAMD 70	vertical	198 kW	2,500	1,581	720	927

The vertical in-line engine shaded grey will mainly be installed as sole engine in a displacement boat, and in semi-displacement and planing boats as a twin-engine installation. Due to asymmetry much more space would be taken up by twin engines because there are no mirror-inverted engines in this power range. A vee engine would therefore be preferable when there is insufficient height for vertical in-line engines.

This six-cylinder in-line Perkins (page 50) is another of the few engines offered in horizontal or vertical form. Single and twin engine installations are compared above. First the dimensions:

Type	Design	Power	Rev/min	Length	Breadth	Height
Perkins HT 6.354M	Horizontal	126 kW	2,400	1,470	1,026	609
Perkins T 6.354M	Vertical	126 kW	2,400	1,422	721	904

The asymmetry of vertical in-line engines (Y) can usually be ignored and amounts here to 35 mm. It is very different when it comes to horizontal engines; asymmetry (X) is far greater and here is 220 mm or about 30% of the breadth of the vertical in-line engine. This has to be taken into account both for single and twin engine installations.

	a	b	c	d	x	y	z*	BS	BH+X	B2S	B2H
Perkins HT			403	623	220				1,246†		2,492‡
Perkins T	343	378				35	170	721		1,612	

*z depends on how the engine is assembled bearing accessibility for maintenance in mind. z here is half a = 170 mm. In twin-engined layouts z is largely decided by asymmetry Y.

†With a single engine the space resulting from asymmetry x can be used for fitting ancillaries such as batteries and pumps. With a twin engined layout the space is lost, amidships at least, because the shafts must leave the hull symmetrically.

‡As engines are not built in mirror-inverted form (only above about 10,000 kW) the breadth required by horizontal twin engines is very great due to asymmetry.

boat engines

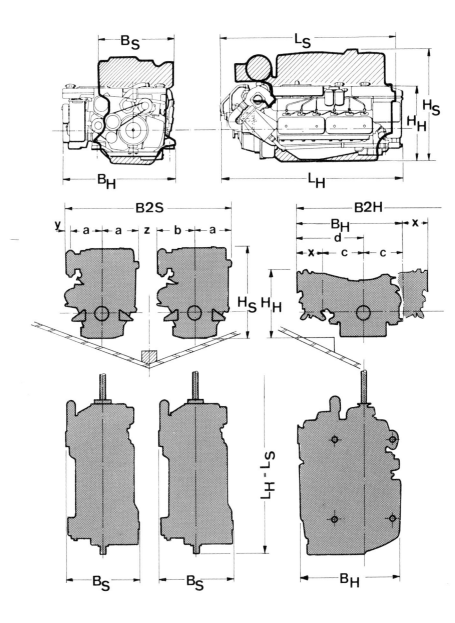

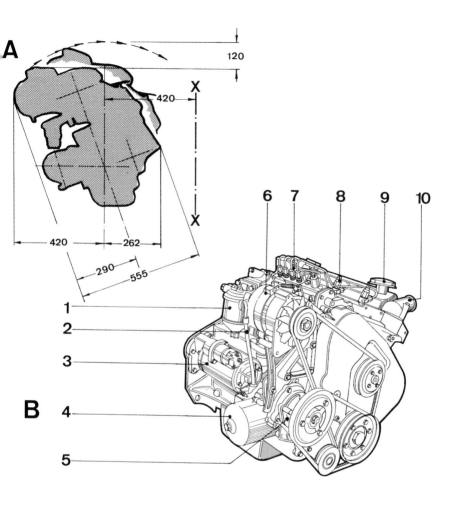

Sketch A: vehicle engines are often installed at an angle and this can be an advantage to the resulting marine conversion as can be seen in this drawing of the Golf diesel. The space lost due to asymmetry can be used for ancillary fittings. The major benefit, however, concerns a completely different matter: the engine is easier to service as can be seen in Sketch B. 1 = fuel filter. 2 = oil dipstick (and change). 3 = starter motor. 4 = oil filter. 5 = water pump. 6 = alternator. 7 = fuel injection pump. 8 = injector. 9 = oil filler cap. 10 = coolant.

boat engines

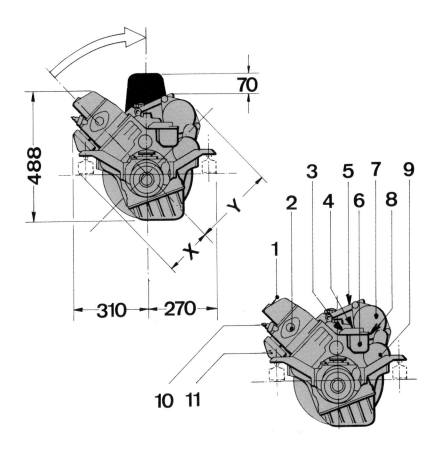

Volvo has even used this method of mounting the engine at an angle for a single-cylinder engine. The advantage is that all fittings attached to the cylinder are easily accessible due to tilting the engine sideways. 1 = decompression handle. 2 = exhaust. 3 = engine speed control. 4 = feed pump and hand priming lever. 5 = cooling water pump. 6 = fuel filter. 7 = alternator. 8 = oil dipstick and oil filter. 9 = starter motor. Only the injector (10) and the air filter (11) lie behind the cylinder head. Anyone who has repaired and serviced an upright engine installed deep under the cockpit will see from this sketch the advantages gained by mounting the engine at an angle.

engine comparisons

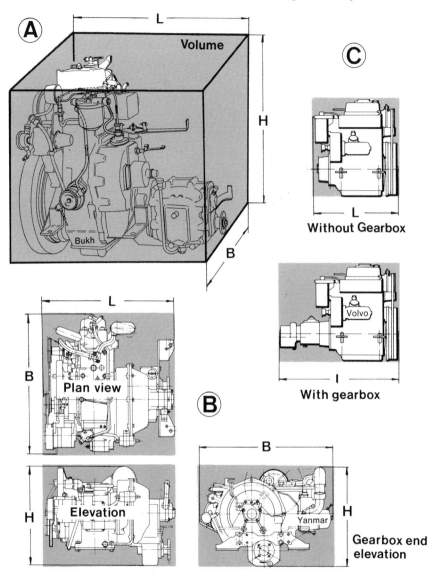

Without Gearbox

With gearbox

Plan view

Elevation

Gearbox end elevation

Here the volume is compared to the actual shape of the engine. The latter can only be established by using scale drawings showing three views of the engine. The length (L), breadth (B) and height (H) measurements, which are multiplied to give the volume, are shaded grey in the dimensional drawings (sketch B).

boat engines

Unfortunately only two drawings are supplied in many cases and the view from above is omitted, but boat engines are generally only seen from above and missing out this view is a considerable handicap for the designer and boatbuilder as well as the buyer.

Sketch C shows how length differs according to whether a gearbox is fitted or not, and this is even clearer in the table on p. 56.

Installation dimensions and volume

Volume, or length × breadth × height, clearly indicates how much space an engine requires. Dimensions are usually given in millimetres, but US and some UK brochures give measurements in inches.

Volume can only be used for purely general comparisons as explained in the previous section on cylinder arrangement. When it comes to the details of evaluating or installing a power unit other factors are important. The boat designer or builder is generally able to use scale drawings showing the engine from above, the side, and either from the front or the back. A proper engine compartment can be laid out using these drawings and detailed measurements, combined with the necessary professional knowledge. This means that the engine will not just squeeze in but that it can be removed for a general overhaul of moving parts, liners etc. Far more important, however, is ease of maintenance, and one of the main concerns of a purchaser should be to check that all points mentioned in the maintenance manual are easy to get at. This depends very largely on how the engine is assembled, and is not merely a question of external dimensions and comparing volume because the dead spaces resulting from the length including gearbox, from incorporating a bend in the exhaust pipe, and from the turbo-charger etc. can always be used for ancillary fittings such as filters, pumps and so on. Points of interest to both designer and buyer are shown in the sketches.

Sketch A: The Ford six-cylinder in-line engine used as an example shows how the height of an engine varies when the angle of installation alters, assuming that the place where the propeller shaft passes through the skin cannot be changed due to hull shape. Three installation angles are shown, 0°, 10° and 15°, and you can see that height H 15° is nearly double H 0°. This is an extreme case, of course, and there are various ways to avoid difficulty, for example as in the figure left where a down-angle shaft is inclined at 8° to the gearbox. Other alternatives are to use an articulated shaft or vee-drive (p. 111). In practice the engine would not be inclined as much as here because point X has been sited as low as possible in the boat and this is what causes the steep angle. It is the outline of the engine, however, that is the determining factor.

Both the next pairs of sketches are included to show how use can be made of engine and oil sump design, and the shape of the gearbox, to site an engine advantageously in the boat.

Sketch B: This in-line six-cylinder Volvo with a very flat sump is particularly suitable for a flat-bottomed boat, and even better suited to a twin-engined layout. If the shaft has to pass through the hull at an angle an articulated shaft

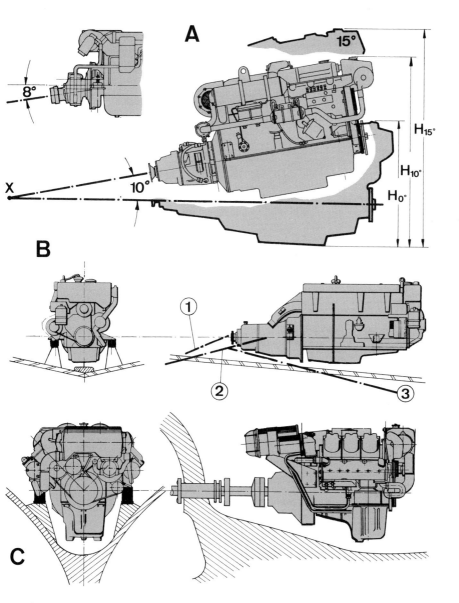

(1) or down-angle drive (2) could be used; alternatively the engine could be installed at an angle in which case the line of the bottom of the hull would follow that of the chain-dotted line numbered 3.

Sketch C: The outline of this six-cylinder WM 6V vee engine makes it especially suitable for certain boats. It can be mounted quite deep in the frame, with the propeller shaft running horizontally, obviously always provided that the boat is suitable.

boat engines

The table below compares several engines, giving their cylinder arrangement (V = vee, L = in-line vertical) and measurements both with and without gearbox (g = gearbox fitted, ng = no gearbox). The areas shaded grey are those where the comparisons are most interesting.

Type	Cylinder No and arrange- ment	Rating B Rev/min	Length A in mm	Breadth B in mm	Height C in mm	Volume A × B × in dm³
Deutz BF 6L 413	6 cyl vee	140/2,650	1,035 ng	1,060	1,002	1,099
Deutz F 6L 413R	6 cyl i-l	122/2,650	1,452 ng	755	1,012	1,109
Farymann S30	2 cyl vee	20–2,500	550 ng 780 g	655	572	206 292
Bukh 20	2 cyl i-l	15/3,000	560 ng 820 g	457	672	172 252
Yanmar 2 QM 20	2 cyl i-l	16/2,700	555 ng 825 g	500	675	187 278
Marine Craft Ford 26 H	6 cyl vee	104/5,500	712 ng 965 g	674	620	297 403
Volvo BB 170A	6 cyl i-l	104/5,000	960 ng 1,392 g	570	660	361 523
MTU 8R	8 cyl i-l	630/1,600	2,730	1,120	1,840	5,626
MTU 16 V	16 cyl vee	1,260/1,600	3,100	1,650	1,870	9,565

Stroke to bore ratio
Current stroke (mm or in) to bore (mm or in) ratios range as follows:
Petrol engines about 0·7:1 to 1·1:1
Diesel engines 0·9:1 to 1·3:1
A ratio below 0·7:1 means a very short stroke engine indeed. A few of this type were built in the sixties but, today, such ratios are only to be found in racing engines where the largest possible valves are required.
As can be seen from the figures above, whereas the bore is greater than the stroke in petrol engines, the diesel tends to have a longer stroke which is greater than the cylinder diameter. Mean piston speed and, with that, the degree of wear to which an engine is subject are directly related to the stroke to bore ratio and engine speed. This is why the slower running diesel engine can have a longer stroke and, within limits, better breathing and gas exchange is the result.

56

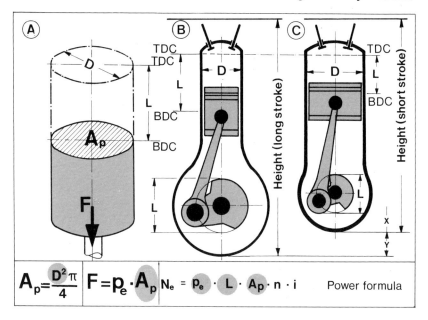

$$A_p = \frac{D^2 \pi}{4} \qquad F = P_e \cdot A_p \qquad N_e = P_e \cdot L \cdot A_p \cdot n \cdot i \qquad \text{Power formula}$$

The sketch here illustrates the stroke to bore ratio and the consequences that result. Sketch A shows the bore, D, the stroke, L, between top dead centre and bottom dead centre, and force F which is applied by the connecting rod to the crankshaft. The greater the area of the piston crown, Ap, or the pressure in the cylinder, the greater the force.

Sketch B shows a typical long stroke engine, and you can see how much higher the cylinder block is than that of the short stroke engine in sketch C. The difference in height is due not only to the shorter piston stroke but to the crank pin's path, the diameter of which must match the stroke. The connecting rod of a short stroke engine can also be reduced in length. Thus the height of the short stroke engine is reduced at the cylinder head and sump by Y, and further by X which varies according to the actual length of the connecting rod. The formulae are shown beneath the three sketches. TDC = top dead centre (or outer dead centre, ODC, for a horizontal engine). BDC = bottom dead centre (or inner dead centre, IDC). D = cylinder diameter or bore, mm². L = stroke, mm. n = rev/min. z = number of cylinders. i = factor.

For example: WM 54 (Mercedes OM 615): stroke 92·4 mm, bore 87 mm: stroke to bore ratio 1·06:1. This ratio of just over 1:1 is typical of recent diesels although they can hardly be described as very long stroke engines. The tendency is to provide a ratio of between 1:1 and 1·3:1. A comparable four-cylinder petrol engine with a similar vehicle rating has a stroke of 65 mm and a bore of 90 mm giving a stroke to bore ratio of 0·72:1. This short stroke engine has a stroke to bore ratio typical of petrol engines.

boat engines

A low stroke to bore ratio means short stroke with large cylinder and piston diameter. A shorter stroke means:

● low mean piston speed because the piston covers a shorter distance.
● lower engine height, not only because the piston stroke is shorter but because the crankcase will be smaller to match the shorter stroke, the connecting rod being attached eccentrically to the crankshaft.
● greater durability because the cylinder walls are less stressed when piston speed is lower.
● larger cylinder diameter. Obviously, if volume is to remain constant, when one factor is reduced the other, in this case the diameter, must be increased.
● large valves. When cylinder diameter is increased there is naturally more space to fit large valves.
● good breathing. More fresh air can enter and more exhaust gases escape in a shorter period.
● higher brake mean effective pressure.

The disadvantages of a short stroke are:

● larger piston diameter (larger surfaces suffer correspondingly greater thermal stresses than smaller surfaces).
● high bearing loading. Pressure in the cylinder works on the piston crown. The higher the pressure the greater the force transmitted by the connecting rod to the bearing.
● the combustion chamber will always be shallower and, with a high compression ratio, this results in poorer combustion.

Piston speeds of current marine engines.

The figure for mean piston speed is so interesting as an almost unqualified measure of the service life of an engine that it is worth taking the trouble to compare the figures. Without mathematical knowledge it is only in this way that you will get on the track of the inter-relationships. Facts come to light which are so surprising that you wonder if there has been a mistake in the calculations. For example your car may idle at about 1,000 rev/min or 16 rev/sec; it has to run this fast if it is to continue ticking over, and without being overloaded at that. Large ships' engines deliver 20,000 kW at an engine speed of one revolution per second (no, that is not a printing error). Also, whereas your car may have a two litre engine the cubic capacity of the largest ships' diesel is as large as your garage. And yet one figure is common to both engines—mean piston speed!

To work through the table: the first two engines are ships' diesels as used for ocean-going vessels. Their output is the same although they are as different as only engines can be. Both weigh about 1 tonne for every ten litres swept volume, and it is worth while comparing all the figures. No conclusions can be drawn as to quality because they have equal claims due to their different applications.

The next engine is listed four times to show the different ratings, and is one of a range of very modern high performance diesels. You can see how very high the mean piston speeds are, but look at the intended applications: 1,000 kW is the overload rating 10% above rating A for cruising engines in multiple installations,

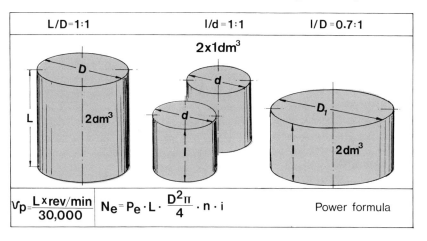

L/D=1:1	l/d = 1:1	l/D = 0.7:1
	$2 \times 1 dm^3$	
$v_p = \dfrac{L \times rev/min}{30,000}$	$N_e = P_e \cdot L \cdot \dfrac{D^2 \pi}{4} \cdot n \cdot i$	Power formula

The sketches show how mean piston speed can be kept low. The same swept volume and the same stroke to bore ratio can be used if the number of cylinders is increased. If the stroke to bore ratio is altered by using a larger bore piston speed will be kept low, but this results in difficulties over gas flow if taken to an extreme (see also stroke to bore ratio).

The formulae are given beneath the sketches. vp = mean piston speed (m/s or ft/min). L = stroke, mm or ft. D = bore, mm² or ins², n = rev/min.

as used in craft such as lifeboats and air-sea rescue boats with high-performance machinery. The rating for yachts and patrol boats is 900 kW at 2,120 rev/min, and you will note that mean piston speed drops immediately. This too is overload rating which means that the engine will only be run for a short time at such a speed. Continuous rating for yachts is given as 760 kW while 660 kW is the rating at the same engine speed but with slightly reduced fuel charge for commercial vessels. Mean piston speed then drops to only 10·3 m/s. The engine would normally be run at about 1,600/1,800 rev/min and piston speed would then be about 8·5 m/s. The same applies to the newly-designed Golf diesel (VW 068.2), and the mean piston speeds are also much the same. Installed in an automobile v_p is about 13·3 m/s at maximum revolutions. Yacht rating B seems to be well selected, 30 kW at 3,600 rev/min, giving a v_p of about 9·6 m/s. With the engine running at about 3,000 rev/min v_p will be about 8 m/s. The same applies to the WM. 54. Next comes a true marine diesel; engine and piston speed is under 8 m/s which should give it great durability, but this engine is used only in commercial craft. The next two engines are supercharged commercial diesel engines used in lorries and other road vehicles; again v_p is about 10 m/s. The last group of four outdrives is included to show that petrol engines have been run with much higher piston speeds for years, although again normal working speed is far below rated speed, and consequently piston speed drops in practice to under 10 m/s.

boat engines

Engine	Type (application)	Rating B kW
Pielstick 20 PC	Ships' diesel	14,000
MAN K 10	Ships' diesel (2-stroke)	14,000
MTU 12 V	Commercial diesel	1,000
	Maximum rating A	900
	Yacht rating	760
	Commercial craft	660
VW-Diesel 068.2	Car (Golf, Passat)	36·7
	Maximum industrial rating B	33·1
	Boat rating B	30·0
WM 54 (OM 615)	Car (Mercedes 220 D)	44
	Yacht rating B maximum	40
	Yacht rating B, 1.6	37
Volvo MD 17 C	True marine diesel	26
Volvo TAMD 70 C	Supercharged commercial diesel (B 1.12)	198
	Normal speed	152
Perkins TV 8.510	Supercharged commercial diesel (B 1.12)	171
	Normal speed	130
Mercruiser V8	Outdrive (4-stroke) Normal speed	206
Chrysler V8	Outdrive (4-stroke) Normal speed	240
Johnson 4	Outdrive (4-stroke) Normal speed	103
Volvo AQ 8V	Outdrive (4-stroke) Normal speed	158

Rev/ min	Stroke mm	Bore mm	Stroke to bore ratio	Mean Piston Speed m/s	No. and arrangement of cyls	Swept Volume dm³
470	520	480	1·08	8·1	20 V	1,882
145	1,250	700	1·78	6·0	10 L	4,810
2,340	155	165	0·94	12·1	12 V	39·7
2,120				10·9		
2,000				10·3		
2,000				10·3		
5,000	80	76·5	1·05	13·3	4 L	1·471
4,000				10·6		
3,600				9·6		
4,200	92·4	87	1·06	12·9	4 L	2·197
3,300				10·2		
3,300				10·2		
2,500	90	88·9	1·01	7·5	3 L	1·680
2,500	130	104·8	1·24	10·8	6 L	6·73
2,200				9·5		
2,600	114	108	1·06	9·9	8 V	8·36
2,400				9·1		
5,000	88·4	101·5	0·87	14·7	8 V	5·72
4,000				11·8		
4,000	95·3	109·8	0·87	12·7	8 V	7·2
3,000				9·5		
4,400	91·5	101·6	0·9	13·4	4 L	2·967
3,500				10·7		
4,400	82·5	98·4	0·84	12·1	8 V	5·02
3,500				9·6		

boat engines

Mean piston speed

The value for mean piston speed is an indication of an engine's mechanical loading. Engine speed cannot be used as a scale for piston speed because it gives no information as to centrifugal force or piston speed. The length of an engine's service life depends to a great extent on mean piston speed and speeds today are restricted to about 17 m/s or 3,346 ft/min with a view to durability. The aim is to keep piston speed relatively low so that wear on cylinder liners and walls is kept to the minimum. The two ways of keeping piston speed down while retaining cylinder capacity unchanged but increasing engine speed are:

1. to increase the number of cylinders. This is expensive and, if carried to excess, engine acceleration would be too rapid.
2. Shortening the stroke and increasing the bore alters the stroke to bore ratio, but this is only possible within certain limits because combustion would then be adversely affected due to reduced breathing capacity (see also stroke to bore ratio, p. 56).

Mean piston speed can be calculated as follows: during one revolution the piston travels twice the length of the stroke; this is multiplied by rev/min to give piston speed. To relate stroke in mm and rev/min to mean piston speed in m/s use the factor 30,000 as below. For piston speed in ft/min multiply stroke by rev/min and divide by 6.

Example: OM 615 (WM 54): 3,300 rev/min at rating B: stroke 92·4 mm.

$$v_p = \frac{L \times n}{30,000} = \frac{92 \cdot 4 \times 3,300}{30,000} = 10 \cdot 16 \text{ m/s or 2,000 ft/min}$$

Maximum output (road rating) is at 4,200 rev/min and mean piston speed is then 12·9 m/s or 2,539 ft/min. Even the new 177 kW Porsche 928 has a v_p of only 13·8 m/s (2,717 ft/min) at maximum engine speed of 5,250 rev/min. Racing engines only exceed 20 m/s (3,937 ft/min) for a very short time if at all. A comparison of marine engines is found on page 61.

Brake mean effective pressure

The value for bmep is obtained by calculation and is arrived at from brake power at appropriate rev/min. The engine designer uses this value with the power formula to determine the main engine measurements, but a man looking at the finished engine can use it to make comparisons.

What do the bmep figures tell us? First it is important that bmep should be greatest not where engine speed is high but where torque is greatest (more on this in the section on engine curves). This is also where combustion is best and fuel is used most economically.

An engine can be properly classified when the limits are known, and these are best found in a standard. Values at present are:

Diesel engines up to about 300 kW $P_e = 60$–90 N/cm² (6–9 bar),
87–130 lbf/in²

Supercharged $P_e = 80$–160 N/cm² (8–16 bar),
116–232 lbf/in²

Petrol engines up to about 300 kW
Normally aspirated $P_e = 70$–110 N/cm² (7–11 bar),
102–160 lbf/in²

Supercharged $P_e = 140 +$ N/cm² (14 bar), 203 lbf/in²

The flexibility of an engine is judged by the difference between highest bmep and bmep at maximum engine revolutions. For an automobile engine flexibility (engine speed range and the difference in power output at maximum torque and maximum revolutions) is a sign of quality, but boat engines should not be too flexible because low torque at high revolutions cause engine speed to fluctuate unnecessarily. A governed engine (low revolutions, high torque) is more suitable for a boat.

$N_e = P_e$	V	z	N
$2N_e = 2P_e$	V	z	N
$2N_e = P_e$	V	$2z$	N
$2N_e = P_e$	$2V$	$\dfrac{3\sqrt{\ }}{z\sqrt{2}}$	$3\dfrac{n}{\sqrt{2}}$
$2N_e = P_e$	$\dfrac{V}{2^3}$	z	$2N$

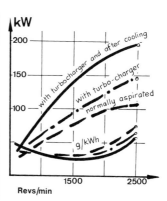

The table above shows clearly which factors are involved when power output is increased. The first line gives the power formula. In the next four lines output is doubled and individual parts of the formula are adapted accordingly. Most convenient is to raise power by increasing bmep. To increase the number of cylinders is a matter for the designer alone. Enlarging cylinder capacity involves altering both the number of cylinders and engine speed; revolutions can only be increased within limits. Increasing the bmep of any given engine is achieved by improving breathing (reducing resistance in the inlet tract) or by supercharging, with a turbo-charger for example. The best example in the diesel engine sector is the 6·7 litre Volvo which, as in the diagram above, delivers 102 kW when normally aspirated and 141 kW when supercharged. When supercharged with aftercooling output rises to 198 kW. This also greatly improves fuel consumption due to the excess air. The lower curves indicate specific fuel consumption.

Looking at the power formula again, engine speed (n) is restricted by mean piston speed (v_p). Bmep (P_e) is limited by air intake (or supercharging) and the quantity of fuel. Capacity (L × A) and the number of cylinders (z) can only be changed by redesigning. The factor (i) is purely the conversion figure. Consequently a high power to weight ratio calls for high specific power output because swept volume is directly related to engine measurements and, therefore, to weight.

boat engines

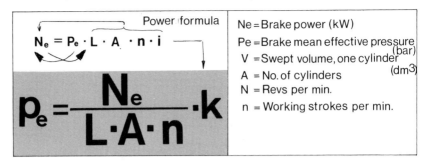

Power formula

$$N_e = P_e \cdot L \cdot A \cdot n \cdot i$$

$$P_e = \frac{N_e}{L \cdot A \cdot n} \cdot k$$

Ne = Brake power (kW)
Pe = Brake mean effective pressure (bar)
V = Swept volume, one cylinder (dm³)
A = No. of cylinders
N = Revs per min.
n = Working strokes per min.

P_e can be calculated by turning the power formula round; every engine's bmep can be checked by inserting the relevant values. Constant i in the power formula is included in the constant k given for the P_e formula and relates to metric measurements.

Output and piston area

Although power related to piston area is a very specialised subject it is important in relation to thermal stresses. What are they? If you look at the power formula (above) again you see that cylinder capacity is one factor involved. The specific power output figures used for making comparisons indicate the amount of power delivered per litre of capacity, and cylinder capacity is piston area times stroke. If the dimension for stroke is omitted and power is related to piston area alone a figure is obtained for power related to the area of the piston and this indicates the degree of thermal stress. This figure gives the number of kW delivered per cm² of piston area. A proper comparison, however, must take into account the shape, cooling and diameter of the piston, how it is made and much else besides so that realistic evaluation requires a very great deal of experience. The values run at about 0·15–0·45 kW/cm².

Like all figures used for comparison, power related to piston area is only of limited interest, in this case because the part which suffers the greatest thermal stress, apart from the piston itself, is the cylinder head area between the valve seatings, and this is the crucial point that limits engine output. The problem is to keep temperature variations in the cylinder head low and so reduce heat-induced compressive stresses which cause fatigue cracks.

Provided this problem is overcome by suitable cylinder head design and piston cooling the same specific power output can be obtained from a diesel (supercharged of course) as from a petrol engine. For example the most powerful diesel today, the Volvo TAMD 70C has a specific power output of nearly 30 kW/dm³. Power related to piston area is 0·38 kW/cm² at rating B 1/12. At maximum output according to DIN 6270 power related to piston area, at 0·46, is greater than the limit just given, and can only be achieved because the pistons are cooled.

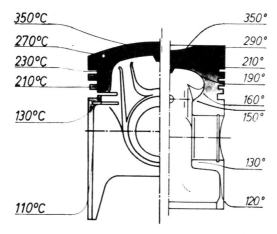

The sketch shows the approximate variations in temperature experienced by a piston under full load (petrol engine right, diesel engine left). It is easy to understand what stresses arise when temperature differs so greatly. (Drawn by K. Schmidt)

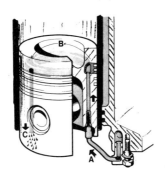

With a given swept volume, the greater the power delivered the greater the thermal load. This affects the piston skirt in particular because this area is more difficult to cool by means of a water-cooled cylinder jacket. The sketch shows a section through a Volvo diesel engine's cylinder with an oil-cooled piston. A = oil jet. B = ring cooling passages in the piston. C = opening through which the oil is sucked back to the sump.

boat engines

Power to weight ratio

The power to weight ratio (kg/kW or lb/hp) gives the number of kilogrammes (lbs) of engine weight per unit of power (kW or hp) delivered to the shaft.

Provided that the design is up to date it can be said, in general, that the higher the revolution rate the lower the power to weight ratio. This is due to the relationship between the number of working strokes and the weight of the engine: i.e. the higher the engine speed the more energy is converted per unit of time. (Naturally this can only be used for comparisons within similar limits because, as already stated, gas exchange deteriorates enormously at very high engine speeds and thermal efficiency is severely reduced—see vehicle rating, Golf-Diesel, p. 73).

Broadly speaking this means lighter in weight, smaller in size, lower costs, less vibration etc. However certain limitations must be borne in mind when assessing the power to weight ratio because underestimating some values can affect the service life of an engine adversely (see mean piston speed).

An exact definition is required, both of the rating and the weight of the engine if a realistic comparison is to be made. It is particularly difficult to define weight accurately when a boat engine is involved because the selection of a particular engine may well involve fitting a certain gearbox, a very special heat exchanger and other extra accessories which are either not required for a different engine or may differ in weight. The best figure to use for comparison is the weight of the dry engine without starter, alternator and batteries etc.

The power to weight ratio has been used as a scale for much wider comparisons than engines alone, and this is best explained by the following example. We shall start with an engine, output 37 kW rating B, installed in a cruiser displacing 10 tonnes, 12 m LOA (40 ft), 10·50 m LWL (34' 6").

● The power to weight ratio varies according to the extent of ancillary fittings etc.

Weight definition	Weight kg	Power/Weight ratio kg/kW*
Bare engine	183	4.9
Vehicle engine, ready for installation	200	5·4
Marine engine without gearbox	234	6·3
Marine engine, with Hurth gearbox	256	6·9
as above plus shaft installation	310	8·4
as above, ready for installation with connections	330	8·9
Ready for use with oil and water	350	9·5
Power to weight ratio of the boat	10,000	270·0

* The first figure for the power to weight ratio is nearly doubled when it comes to the engine ready for use. This is why a very exact definition of weight is essential when making comparisons. This is equally true of output rating as shown below:

● The power to weight ratio varies according to the output rating definition. Basic weight of the marine engine quoted above, without gears, is 234 kg.

Rating definition	rev/min	Output	Power/weight ratio
Vehicle rating (DIN 70020)	4,200	44	5·3
Rating B (DIN 6270)	3,300*	37	6·3
Continuous rating A (DIN 6270)	3,300*	33	7·1

* Here too the ratio varies greatly even when only these three DIN definitions are used, each of which is quoted as brake power according to the intended application. The increase in output here is not due to an alteration in engine speed but to increased flow rate (through improved breathing and the injection of more fuel). Output is limited at rating B, the overload rating above continuous rating A.

Some engines are listed below for comparison: the same basis has been used for all the weights.

Type of engine	Power kW	Rev/min	Swept volume dm³	Power/ Weight kg/kW	Spec. power output kg/dm³	No and arrangement of cyls	Weight kg
Real marine diesel	15	2,500	1·5	12–15	10–15	L 2 N	200
VW diesel	33	4,000	1·5	6·0	22·0	L 4 N	200
Volvo 70	78	2,500	6·7	10·3	11·6	L 6 N	800
Volvo 70T	141	2,500	6·7	5·7	21·0	L 6 T	800
Volvo 70TA	198	2,500	6·7	4·0	29·5	L 6 TA	800
Perkins 6·3	85	2,800	5·8	6·5	14·6	L 6 N	550
Perkins 6·3T	105	2,400	5·8	6·2	18·1	L 6 T	650
Perkins 6·3G	126	2,600	5·8	5·3	21·7	L 6 TA	670
WM 130T	115	2,800	5·7	4·3	20·2	L 6 T	500
WM 240	188	2,500	12·7	4·9	14·8	V 8 N	920
Petrol engines	100	5,000	3·0	3·0	33·3	L,V 4 N	300
Petrol engines	200	5,000	6·0	3·0	33·3	L,V 6/8 N	600
Special petrol engines	200	6,500	4·0	1·0	50·0	L,V 6/8 N	200

The figures above relate only to the engine and give an indication as to how the raw materials are used.

The term power to weight ratio can be extended and the figures are more readily understood if the figures are related to the whole boat. Given a figure of 500 kg/kW no-one will be in doubt as to whether a planing boat or a displacement boat is involved. Equally when the figure is 10 kg/kW it will be obvious whether it is a planing boat or not. These two last figures force you to a conclusion which is less familiar. Turn these facts round to estimate the power required for a boat and you can say, roughly, 500 kg/kW $\doteq$ 2 kW/t and 10 kg/kW $\doteq$ 100 kW/t (see power estimation).

$$N_e = P_e \cdot L \cdot A \cdot n \cdot i$$

boat engines

Specific power output or the power to volume ratio

The figure for specific power output gives information about loading and capacity and is therefore useful when making comparisons. Although for decades ever higher specific power output has been achieved, among other things due to taxation based on cubic capacity, there has been a noticeable break in this trend since 1973, mainly on account of regulations concerning exhaust pollution but also as a result of rethinking with regard to service life and economy.

Today specific power output figures as follows are general:

Diesel engines up to about 250 kW (335 hp)	13–30 kW/dm³
Petrol engines (automobile)	22–50 kW/dm³
Racing engines	up to 110 kW/dm³

See also engines and the power formula left.

Number of cylinders

A large number of cylinders results in constant torque and very good engine balance. Multi-cylinder engines are quiet and free from vibration but are more expensive. Even if the difference is not so marked in the purchase price, maintenance costs are higher because every extra cylinder increases the cost of spare parts, e.g. six instead of four plugs etc.

● Normally the number of cylinders is:

Motor cycles	1–2
Outboard engines	1–6 in-line and vee
Automobiles	4–8 in-line and vee
Lorries	6–8 in-line and vee
Ships' diesels and stationary engines	8–20 vee, 1–12 in line

See also piston speed, stroke to bore ratio, engine data and the power formula (page 67).

Engine curves

These days a full load power curve is provided for almost every boat engine, and is virtually part and parcel of even a cheap brochure. The values entered are those delivered at the test bench with the engine under full load, naturally allowing for any deviation permitted in the standard. There are three curves which relate to power output, torque and specific fuel consumption, but many marine engine graphs also include the propeller law curve. Many conclusions about an engine and its behaviour can be drawn from these curves.

The propeller law curve is purely theoretical and is based on the fact that a propeller's power requirement increases as a cubic parabola. Power absorption by the propeller affects fuel consumption, but to what extent is a question left unanswered by almost all engine manufacturers. Fuel consumption at partial load does not match that at full load. Boat engines are only a small part of a manufacturer's total output, and because a partial load fuel consumption curve would be just as theoretical as the propeller law curve they are both omitted. It would, however, be well worth the trouble to include this curve, however theoretical, when boat engine pamphlets are reprinted.

We shall be using values from a rather idealised Mercedes performance graph which also serves as the starting point for partial load values and statements in later chapters.

Engine curves are just like other diagrams in that:
- the values and test standard conditions must be exactly defined or they will be of little use, and
- the reader must be able to interpret them.

On the following pages you will find a number of engine curves which, it is true, require a little technical understanding if they are to be interpreted, but the compensation will be a better understanding of your engine, and this will almost automatically lead to fewer repairs and to the expectation of longer engine life.

Full load curves are usually provided. All values relate to brake power at full load, i.e. at all engine speeds the maximum amount of fuel required for combustion is received (thus, diesel engines to the limit when smoke becomes visible in the exhaust).

The horizontal scale shows engine speed in rev/min while the vertical scale indicates the figures relevant to what is being measured, namely power, torque or specific fuel consumption. The figures on the left relate to SI units and those on the right to the British units used hitherto.

As a propeller (propeller law) does not absorb anything approaching the full output of an engine except under certain particular circumstances, the curves are useful mostly for making comparisons. The example shows how to interpret them; if you require the values at a certain engine speed find the relevant rev/min on the engine speed scale (A–A), and follow this up vertically to the appropriate curve (D, C, B). Move horizontally to the vertical scale and read off the answers at G, F and E.

Various full load curves are printed on the pages which follow to show what inferences can be drawn from these 'test bench' curves as to the character of the engine. From top to bottom they all indicate power, torque and specific fuel consumption, related in each case to engine speed.

Sketch A: If combustion continued to be as efficient at higher engine speeds as at I the power curve would continue to point 1 as a straight line. Beyond a certain point after maximum torque fuel flow (gas exchange) deteriorates, the rate of increase of every engine's power output slows down, and the curve drops down to 2. This effect is so marked that, beyond a certain engine speed, the full load curve would drop away even further to point 3 and towards 4. This is described technically as reduction in thermal efficiency.

When evaluating an engine remember that there is no such thing as a full load curve that runs straight. Although a straight line is often used to indicate full load in construction and agricultural machinery pamphlets this merely indicates that the engine was not brake tested, and that the graph has been drawn with the final point determined purely by calculation. Values at lower speeds would then lie above the straight line, as shown by the thin broken line, a. If this were not so the engine would be unable to produce the maximum power output shown.

boat engines

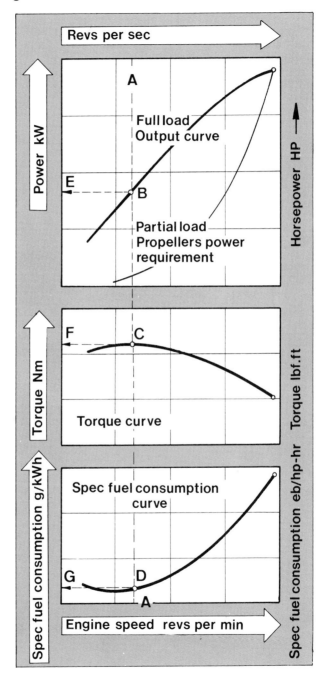

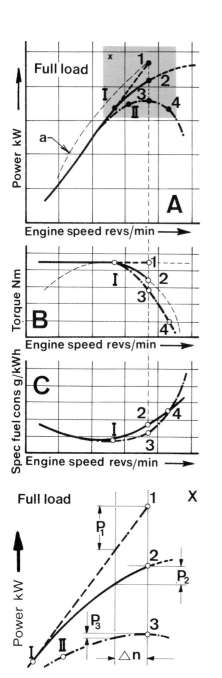

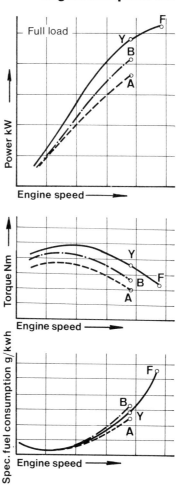

boat engines

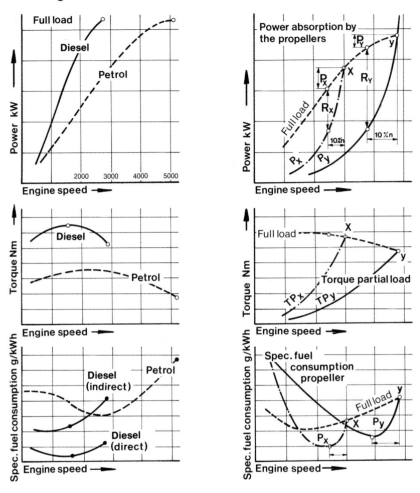

The degree of bend at the top end of the curve shows how closely the engine's maximum output approaches the figure declared by the manufacturer. Yacht rating B would lie roughly at point 2 and that of a different engine plotted as a dotted curve at point II. Point 3 gives a rough indication of maximum vehicle output.

Sketch B: Theoretically torque, as a ratio of power to engine speed, should be a horizontal line but in practice is a curve with its highest point at medium engine speed where brake mean effective pressure is highest. The labelling in the diagram matches that of the full load curve. The torque curve is not particularly informative for boats. In cars it indicates the degree of flexibility of the engine (how long you can stay in one gear without changing). The dash-dotted curve (3 and 4) indicates greater flexibility and more comfortable driving than curve 2; the latter is preferable for boats.

Sketch C: Specific fuel consumption is inversely proportional to torque and therefore curves the opposite way. This curve indicates the efficiency of the combustion. In the maximum torque range, where combustion is best (highest bmep), least fuel is burnt to deliver 1 kWh. When different engines are compared the curves show which is the most economical, and here engine 3 is more economical than engine 2. If, however, you look at II you find confirmation of the fact stated above that II corresponds to the power output of 2, and also delivers 1 kW with the same quantity of fuel. When using this curve remember that it indicates the amount of fuel required to deliver one kW at varying rates of engine revolutions. This means that, when at full load (careful, this is important) the engine will be working most economically where the curve is lowest. In a boat the most economical range will lie elsewhere on the propeller law curve (partial load).

The area shaded grey is enlarged below to demonstrate what happens when power output is limited at different points. Although engine speed increases by the same amount, n, (for example n = 200 rev/min) the rate of increase in power output differs. The higher the engine speed the lower the rate of increase. The rate also slows as the engine approaches the point, at full load, beyond which combustion becomes poor or bad. Compare the lengths of P1, P2 and P3 which show how much power output rises while engine speed increases by the same amount (Δ_n).

These are power outputs in accordance with DIN standards. F = maximum vehicle rating—DIN 70020. Y = maximum yacht rating—DIN 6270: corresponds to maximum effective output. The point lies on the DIN 70020 vehicle power curve, power being raised by improved breathing and the injection of a greater quantity of fuel. Output is limited. B = rating B—DIN 6270: corresponds approximately to the permissible 10% overload above continuous rating A. Output is limited. A = continuous rating A—DIN 6270: 10% overloadable and only limited when overloaded (110%).

The torque and specific fuel consumption curves show clearly how the outputs were obtained: vehicle rating F through higher engine speed, a corresponding increase in specific fuel consumption and greatly improved breathing (different filters).

Yacht rating Y is higher than normal rating B, and falls in the category 'maximum effective output that can be developed by an engine depending on its application during a certain period'.

Curves A and B also result from differences in fuel flow and breathing; i.e. torque and specific fuel consumption vary according to how the engine is tuned to deliver a certain brake power.

Comparing diesel and petrol engines.
Three major differences stand out clearly here:
1. On average the petrol engine's revolution rate is almost double that of the diesel—diesel 2,500–3,000 rev/min, petrol 5,000–6,000 rev/min. The

73

boat engines

diesel's lower engine speed increases propeller efficiency but this difference can be cancelled out by fitting reduction gear, although that also involves a larger, heavier gearbox.

2. The torque curves arise from the ratio of power to engine speed. At high engine speed torque is low, and vice versa. The diesel's torque is greater and, in the early years of outdrives, this resulted in premature wear to the gear teeth surfaces. The propeller benefits greatly from higher torque.

3. The specific fuel consumption curves show clearly that the diesel engine is more economical. The bend in the second third of the petrol engine's curve is caused by the carburettor and, depending on the type of engine, this may occur at higher or lower engine speeds. The direct injection diesel's lower specific fuel consumption is a very important point. Although the engine may be rougher and noisier in use due to much higher ignition pressure the indirect injection diesel engine's greater specific fuel consumption makes it much less economical when working hours are long and power output is high.

	Indirect injection spec. fuel consumption		Direct injection spec. fuel consumption	
Rev/min %	Full load g/kWh	Partial load g/kWh	Full load g/kWh	Partial load g/kWh
100	300	300	252	252
90	300	278	240	230
80	290	278	237	230
70	285	285	235	235
60	285	290	236	240
50	285	300	240	255
40	290	325	242	270
30	300	380	250	285

The table gives full and partial load fuel consumption figures for diesel engines with direct and indirect injection. The partial load values for indirect injection have been estimated using the performance graph on p. 76.

engine comparisons

Although the curves on the previous pages provided no information directly useful for boats they do give an insight into the behaviour of an engine. Now come curves which are found but rarely in engine leaflets.

The broken line is the full load curve of two diesel engines. Both curves end at the yacht ratings declared by the manufacturer, X and Y. The propeller law curves, P_X and P_Y, which indicate the amount of power absorbed by the propeller at varying engine speeds, are drawn through these points.

The vertical distance between the full load and propeller law curves is reserve power, R, which is the difference between the power that could be delivered by the engine at this revolution rate as compared to the actual power absorbed. As can be seen the engines are under full load only at the end of the curves at X and Y, when engine speeds are highest and the propellers absorb the engines' full power output. At all other speeds the engines are under partial load, and this is a state when an engine does not always work particularly economically (see the diesel performance graph on p. 76.

At point X engine X's full load curve still runs relatively straight whereas, at point Y, that of engine Y has flattened considerably. The propeller law curve of both engines is a cubic parabola. The difference in inclination of the two power curves indicates that the two engines are under different loads as can be seen by comparing R_X and R_Y when both engines are running at 10% less than their respective rated speeds. These two engines are compared again on p. 76 and you will see there that engine X's propeller (P_X) is working in a far better range than engine Y's propeller (P_Y). This is because engine X is operating at a lower specific load and combustion is more economical (distance between maximum power and maximum torque); at maximum output engine Y is a fair distance away from the range where bmep is highest. If the propeller law curve ended at point X engine Y would achieve the same specific condition as engine X; this means selecting engine output so that the curve indicating the propeller's absorption of power and the full load curve coincide at a point nearer to the maximum torque range (see also Power estimation and Propeller efficiency). The torque and specific consumption curves show that engine X is the more economical.

This is the rather idealised performance graph of a vehicle diesel engine with indirect injection. The top full load curve relates to rating B while the full load curve entered below it approximates to continuous rating A. The grey area shows the course of the propeller law curve, which indicates the propeller's partial load power requirements. The upper limit of the grey area relates to the propeller of a planing boat and the lower limit to that of a displacement boat.

To interpret the performance graph, first follow the hyperbolae which indicate similar power output; these are given as percentages of maximum output. If, for example, you follow the line showing 40% of maximum power (a) you will see the course of partial load power absorption. In other words, if you were to require full power when the engine was running at 40% of maximum revolution rate this would correspond to about 40% of maximum load (A). The engine would be most economical at 30–40% of maximum output, running at about 50% of maximum engine speed (Z). If the engine speed were increased but no more than 40% power demanded specific fuel consumption would rise

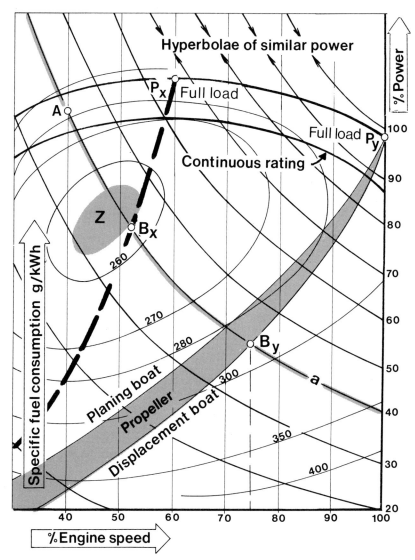

Hyperbolae of similar power

P_x Full load

A

Full load P_y

100

Continuous rating

90

80

Z

B_x

260

70

Specific fuel consumption g/kWh

% Power

270

60

280

B_y

50

Planing boat

Propeller

300

a

40

Displacement boat

350

30

400

20

40 50 60 70 80 90 100

% Engine speed

gradually from Z until finally about 360 g/kWh would be used at 100% or maximum revolutions. The propeller's requirement for power from the engine follows a very different course as engine speed increases. When the revolution rate is low the propeller requires very little power indeed but calls for maximum power at high speed, passing through a partial load area where, although specific fuel consumption alters less violently than when following the hyperbolae of similar power, the results are poor as to economical engine speeds. This can also be seen in the figures in the table of page 74.

engine comparisons

Comparing six diesel engines. Imagine that, depending on the amount of power required, these could be installed as the power unit of a cruiser about 40 ft (12 m) in length. To increase the variation for comparison purposes, the power of the Volvo and the Fiat have been increased by adding a fourth cylinder. Engine data will be found in the table below. The letters in the diagrams mean F = Fiat, G = VW Golf, M = Mercedes, V = Volvo, while the 4 indicates that a fourth cylinder has been added.

From top to bottom the diagrams show power output, specific fuel consumption and hourly consumption. The curves on the left relate to full load, and those on the right to a propeller fitted to a displacement boat.

Note the following points: F4 almost matches the vehicle rating of the Mercedes (44 kW) but uses almost 5 l/h or just over 1 gallon (over 25%) less fuel. It is, however, a direct injection engine, almost twice as heavy and much noisier. The same is true when the VW Golf diesel engine (vehicle rating 37 kW) is compared with the Fiat and the Volvo 4. The boat would have adequate power if the Volvo MD 17C were fitted. Note particularly the course of the consumption curves on the right. This is covered more fully in the chapter on consumption.

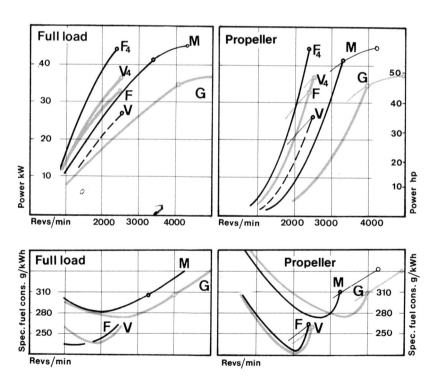

boat engines

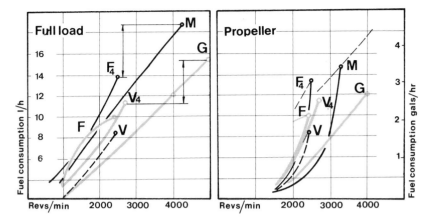

Engine	Rating DIN B kW	Rev/min	Bore mm	Stroke mm	Swept Volume dm³
VW 068.2	33	4,000	76·5	80	1·471
Mercedes OM 615	40	3,300	87	92·4	2·197
Volvo MD 17C	26	2,500	88·9	90·0	1·680
Volvo MD 17/4	35	2,500	88·9	90·0	2·240
Fiat 8035M	32	2,400	100	110	2·590
Fiat 8035/4	43	2,400	100	110	3·450

Weight	Power Weight Ratio kg/kW	spec. power output kW/dm³	max torque/ rev/m	Cyl No./ Injection	
180*	5·5	22·4	82/3,000	4	i
260	6·5	18·2	121/2,100	4	i
290	11·2	15·5	108/2,200	3	d
350†	10·0	15·6	121/2,200	4	d
380	11·8	12·4	145/1,500	3	d
460‡	10·7	12·4	152/1,500	4	d

*The weight of the VW industrial engine 068.2 Golf is given as 129 kg but when converted for marine use and a gearbox added weight would amount to about 180 kg.
†The Volvo MD 17/4 is based on the three-cylinder engine and is purely invented so that a comparison can be made with a four-cylinder engine. The weight is roughly estimated.
‡The same holds good for the Fiat 8035/4

i = indirect
d = direct

2. Engine installation— considerations and comparisons

All well-known engine manufacturers, and those who convert vehicle engines for marine purposes, either provide very detailed and, generally, excellent printed instructions on installation or are ready to offer advice on the subject. Why is it then that, after the engine has been installed in the boat, only part of the engine's power output, as given on the type data plate, is actually delivered to the shaft? The usual cause is a chronic shortage of air leading to an overheated engine compartment.

Although this can easily be proved mathematically it is even easier in practice; raise the lid of the engine compartment and the engine starts to run better. A diesel stops being smelly, and a petrol engine runs faster. However, insufficient air is only the most common fault when installing engines in series-produced boats. When yachts are to be built in larger numbers the major problems should be resolved as effectively as possible because, for example, a large hole costs no more than a small hole, and to lead an intake duct correctly from the start involves no extra expenditure. Many annoying faults are found, and boat builders will only take note as a result of pressure from owners.

What is required from a boat engine once it has been installed?
1. It should be able to perform at its best and reliably, but require the minimum of maintenance and repairs.
2. It should take up as little space as possible.
3. It should be as inconspicuous as possible with regard to sight, feeling, smell and hearing.

That is the broad outline of what is desirable and, although these three requirements are interlinked, we shall consider them in turn.

Optimum performance with minimal maintenance and care
Faultless servicing and care are essential if repairs are to be kept to the minimum. This calls for an engine compartment of adequate size, while certain parts of the engine must be readily accessible. No general guidelines can be laid down because every make of engine is different and the details have to be decided by the designer, or are supplied to the boatyard by the engine manufacturer. The sketches on p. 85/6 show how the measurements are determined.

An installed engine will only deliver full power if it is able to do so. In other words an installed 100 kW engine, for example, will only deliver 100 kW when atmospheric conditions are the same as when it was bench tested, namely temperature 20°C, humidity 60% and air pressure 981 mbars for a DIN 6270

boat engines

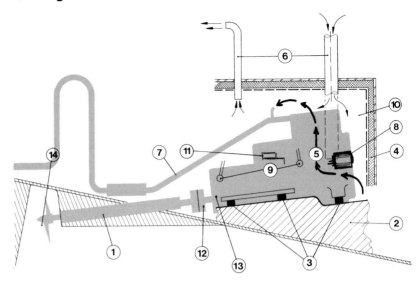

This general sketch shows the various parts of an engine installation as discussed in the following pages: 1 = stern tube and shaft installation. 2 = engine bed. 3 = flexible engine mountings. 4 = sound proofing. 5 = cooling. 6 = engine compartment air inlet and extraction ducts. 7 = exhaust system. 8 = electrical installation. 9 = gear and engine speed controls. 10 = engine compartment. 11 = fuel system. 12 = coupling. 13 = gearbox. 14 = propeller.

rating. These conditions alter when the engine is installed in the boat, and always for the worse which means that an engine always has to perform on board in less favourable conditions than at the test bench. How much performance is reduced depends on the design of the engine compartment and, above all, on how efficiently air is supplied and extracted.

If the engine compartment is so well laid out that no noticeable drop in air pressure is caused by the intake of air for combustion purposes the engine will deliver its power, always provided that the combustion air is not overheated in the engine compartment to such a degree that, again, power output would be affected. In practice this means that large section inlet and outlet ducts are required to provide air both for combustion and for engine compartment ventilation.

The 20°C specified for a bench test rating is certainly not a practical proposition, and will be altered to 40°C in DIN 6271. An engine should therefore be selected that is powerful enough to meet the propeller's requirements when the engine compartment's temperature is about 40°C. The power delivered at 20°C reduces by about 10% when combustion air temperature is about 40°C and the installed 100 kW engine will then only deliver 90 kW due to the increased temperature of the combustion air.

An engine not only produces heat which is dissipated by cooling water but heats air by radiation, and therefore raises the temperature in the engine compartment. The degree of heat varies because, for example, raw water cooled engines (direct cooling) run at about 60°C whereas engines with closed cooling circuits run with a cooling water temperature of 80–100°C, depending on overpressure.

The heat radiated and transmitted to the air warms the engine compartment and the engine therefore sucks in warmer air unless air for combustion purposes is fed to it separately.

In practice engines up to about 50 kW take air direct from the engine compartment (see p. 92) whereas for higher output engines the aim is to provide a separate supply of combustion air, using a different ventilation system to cool the compartment itself. There is much to be said in favour of both methods and every case should be considered independently to decide which is preferable. A middle course is possible because two air ducts are advisable anyway; one can be led directly to the engine's air intake filter while the second exhausts air from the bilges of a petrol-engined boat or from the highest point of a diesel's engine compartment.

The size of the ducts depends on power output and the amount of heat radiated by the engine, and the details are given by the engine manufacturer.

The next point to consider, if maximum output is to be delivered, is to install the engine, together with gearbox and shafting, as faultlessly as possible. Alignment is the greatest problem because even slight inaccuracy quickly damages bearings and the stern tube packing. For further details see p. 97.

Economy of space
This sounds so easy but is very difficult in practice. Whatever the engine that has been chosen for its particular characteristics, such as specific power output or cylinder arrangement, even the choice of the sound-absorption materials used affects the amount of space required for the engine compartment because sound-absorbent lining varies from 20–80 mm thick, and that will mean about 80 mm for the two sides anyway. However a far more important factor than this 80 mm exterior measurement is the overall amount of space required for the engine compartment itself and, although this varies for every individual engine, the guideline is that the compartment must be large enough for maintenance to be carried out without dismantling the engine or dislocating joints. Laying up for the winter should be possible without too much difficulty, and smaller repairs should be feasible without having to take the engine or half the compartment to pieces. In other words, if the oil has to drain into the bilges when it is being changed because there is no room to hold a container beneath the sump and no alternative arrangement is provided, sooner or later you will be tempted not to change the oil or to leave longer intervals between changes. This is equally true, of course, of the gearbox, shafting and all ancillary fittings such as pumps and batteries.

boat engines

Unobtrusiveness—sight, hearing, feeling and smell
This is the designer's concern, but unobtrusiveness should not be carried to such an extreme that seats, steps etc. have to be removed before the engine can be got at.

Engine, gearbox, shaft, propeller, flexible mountings and the engine cradle should all be mutually attuned. The expertise of the yard is largely responsible for overcoming vibration. Resonance over a broad range of engine speed, caused by various independent vibrations of the individual parts, is particularly unpleasant and will only be observed by a purchaser during a thorough trial run.

Overcoming noise is another question for which the designer is largely responsible. Attempts to reduce noise level at a later stage are generally expensive. If the engine compartment is as air-tight as possible, and the air inlet and outlet ducts are properly arranged, the smell from the engine compartment will be dispersed in the open air, with the help of an extractor fan if necessary.

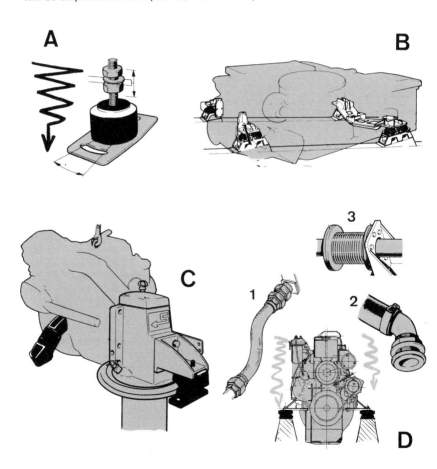

Below

A: the engine bed has to be resistant to torque and must distribute as widely as possible over the hull all the forces which stem from the engine. Propeller forces also have to be allowed for when they are absorbed by the gearbox direct, rather than the thrust and shear forces being distributed through a separate thrust block.

B: section through a glassfibre bed. The black rectangle is an embedded steel bar into which the bolt of the bonded rubber mounting is screwed. If flexible mountings are not used the hatched hollow space should not be filled with foam but with material such as sand and plastic to absorb vibration.

C: section through a wooden bed.

D: section through a steel bed. This should be so constructed that the forces are distributed by stringers which run longitudinally. The floors which run athwartships only increase resistance to torque.

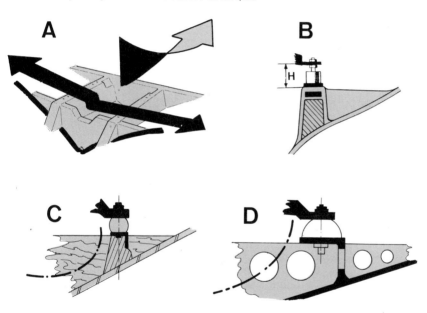

Left

Boat engines are always suspended on flexible mountings. This damps vibration and increases comfort enormously. Bonded rubber pads (A) are used. B shows a horizontal six-cylinder engine suspended on four mountings. C is a three-point mounting for a sail-drive. Outdrives are similarly mounted.

Figure D: because the engine is suspended on flexible mountings it moves in relation to its surroundings. Flexible connections and cables are therefore needed for all lines leading to and from the engine for fuel, coolant, electrical fittings and exhaust. 1 = reinforced hose. 2 = spiral or woven hose. 3 = compensator.

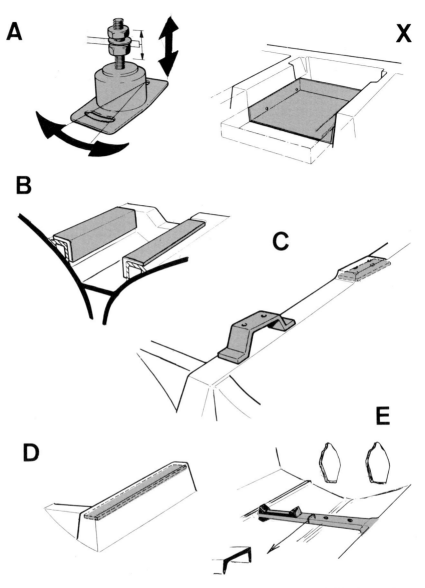

A mounting similar to the Volvo mounting (A) is most suitable for engine alignment. B: a steel bracket is often added as reinforcement and should be laminated in to series production boats. C: brackets, the nearer is adjustable and the further is laminated in; these also make alignment easier. D: flat metal reinforcing bar, laminated in. E: the cradle for twin outdrives looks as simple as this. Prefabricated brackets with elongated holes are attached to a metal cross member mounted on two stringers. X: collecting tray for spilt engine oil.

84

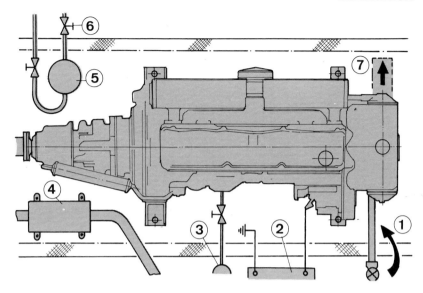

A slim, in-line engine in a narrow engine compartment. Note several points which show that the installation layout has been poorly conceived. 1 = whenever possible sea-water filter and sea-cocks should be in the engine compartment, not only to encourage a more frequent inspection of the engine but also to avoid having to open and close other stowage areas in addition to the engine compartment. 2 = batteries up to 2 kW can be stowed in the engine compartment. The heavy leads, starter and power cables will have shorter runs and can therefore be of smaller cross-section. 3 = fuel filters should be in the engine compartment. 4 = the heater is correctly postioned in as much as it draws in heating air from the cockpit. 5 = the water pump and valves (6) should be in the engine compartment, or at least both in the same area. 7 = the heat exchanger has to be completely removed for cleaning because there is too little space to withdraw the tube stack.

Over: these are some of the main measurements and installation problems; they vary according to the boat. Sailing boat cockpits are about 600 mm wide, and this causes problems if the engine is broad. A second important measure: the engine compartment should be no deeper than 800 mm unless there is space for the shoulders and chest. About 200 mm should be left clear either side of the engine (spanners).

Space poses less problems in the case of an outdrive; when the hinged cover is raised the engine is completely accessible.

boat engines

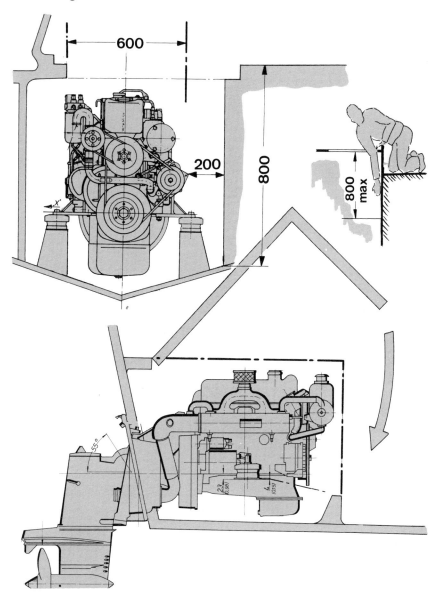

Below: Details of the seawater cooling circuit. 1 = strainer at inlet. The slots are placed forward in motor boats but aft in sailing boats. 2 = sea-cock close by the hull; also illustrated are a rapid-closing lever-operated sea-cock and a screw-down gate valve which can be raised and lowered (better value). 3 = seawater filter; there are many varieties but gauze filters are always used. 4 = synthetic rubber hose. Warning: do not use normal PVC tubing. 5 = flexible connection to the engine if all fittings so far are rigid.

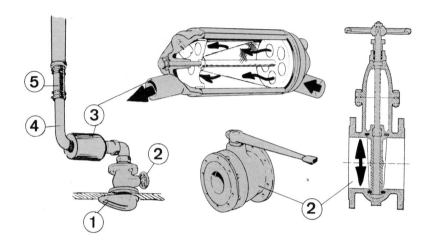

Over: the more usual cooling systems.
A: direct or seawater cooling. 1 = sea-cock. 2 = seawater filter. 3 = flexible connections. 4 = outlet with the exhaust piping. 5 = water-lock system if the cylinder head is too deep in the boat (see exhaust p. 95).
B: Air cooling: No cooling water circuit is needed which is an advantage, but a great deal of air is required (disadvantage).
C: Indirect cooling: This is essential for all converted automobile, lorry and industrial engines because, unlike true boat diesels, they suffer badly from salt water. Heat exchanger cooling is shown here (keel cooling on the following pages). The closed circuit engine coolant is recooled in the heat exchanger (4) by the raw water circuit (1–5). The heat exchanger is shown in greater detail on the right: a = housing. b = tube stack; black arrows indicate seawater, grey arrows show engine cooling circuit.

boat engines

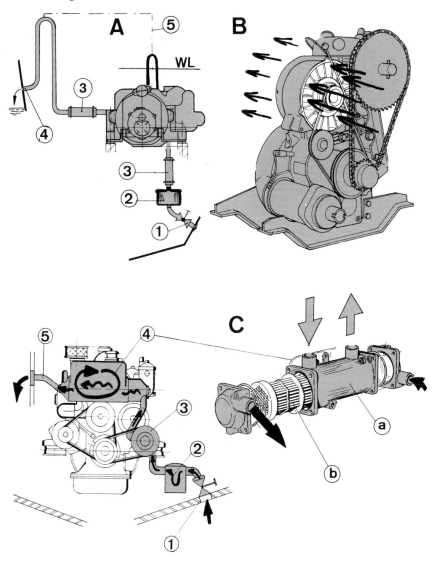

Keel cooling. Theoretically this is the most reliable cooling system for water-cooled engines because without an open circuit (raw water) no blockages can occur and no corrosion arise in the normal sense of the word. Whereas skin-tank cooling can only be used for metal-hulled vessels keel cooling is possible for boats of all materials, but is only used for displacement boats because it both increases the wetted area of planing boats and causes turbulence.

The disadvantages of this outboard heat exchanger are marine fouling, the need for paint and poor exchange of heat when raw water temperatures are high and also at lower speeds although engine loading may be higher, in head winds for example.

Sketch A shows the main alternatives. 1 = the keel itself acts as the heat exchanger. 2 = pipes fitted either side of the keel. 3 = pipes fitted at the chines.

Sketch B: cross section through the closed cooling circuit. Above the keel pipe (1) the pump (2) sucks up the coolant water, forces it through the header tank (3) in which the tube stack would otherwise be fitted, through the pipe (4) to the second keel pipe (5). The circuit is completed by the return cross pipe (6).

Sketch C: this skin-tank is virtually a box welded to the hull through which the coolant is pumped back and forth. The water streaming past on the outside of the hull extracts heat from the coolant. The breadth (B) and height (H) of the chambers are decisive.

Although the general view is that a large area of tubes is required to exchange heat by this method, calculations as to the size of keel pipes or skin-tanks establish that this is not so. Generally speaking two pipes about 75% of the boat's length with a diameter of 0·5 mm/kW are sufficient for displacement boats with normal engines. The size of a skin-tank required for a moderately powered boat such as a sailing boat is so small that, for example, the rudder surface is adequate to dissipate engine heat. (This cooling method was patented by K. W. Schröter, yacht designer). Although those opposed to keel cooling are partially justified, keel and skin-tank cooling are preferable in dirty waters with a muddy bottom and in shallow sandy areas. There is no danger of the engine overheating if the dimensions are calculated correctly.

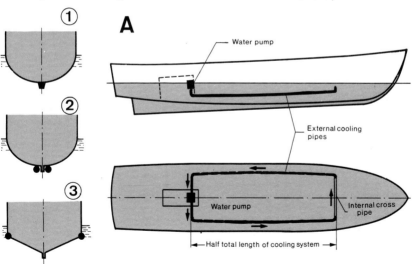

① ② ③ **A**

Water pump

External cooling pipes

Water pump   Internal cross pipe

Half total length of cooling system

boat engines

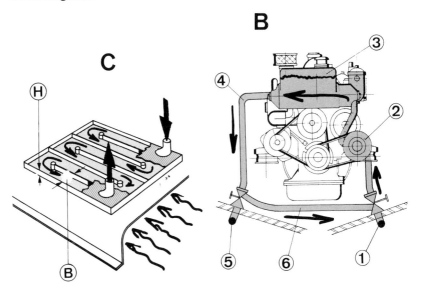

The sketches below and right show how engine compartments for low and medium output engines are normally ventilated. Because the water-cooled engine gives off heat through convection and radiation the engine compartment itself must be kept cool, as well as the combustion air. Otherwise the warmer intake air will cause output to drop (see chapter on power).

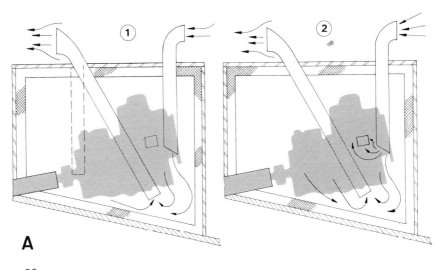

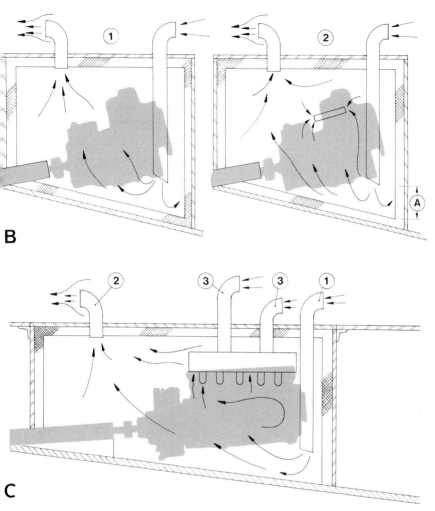

These pages show how much trouble is taken over the provision of cool combustion air.

A: this is the ventilation layout for a small petrol engine, shown at rest (1) and working (2). While the engine lies idle air circulates naturally in the compartment, leading all gases, and especially the heavy explosive gases, outboard. This is why the outlet duct starts close above the lowest point of the bilges. The inlet duct ends just forward of the carburettor so that when the engine is running it receives cool fresh air. As a rough guide the cross-section area of the inlet duct should be large enough to supply four to five times the amount of air required for combustion.

boat engines

B: ventilation layout for a small diesel engine installation, 1 at rest, 2 running. Unlike the petrol engine the inlet duct ends at A about 200–300 mm above the lowest point of the bilges, and not at the air filter. The outlet duct starts at the highest point of the compartment so as to suck out the maximum amount of heated air. This is possible when diesel oil is used because the gases are less dangerous.

C: for larger engines over 50 kW the supply of cool air for the engine compartment is separate from that of combustion air. 1 and 2 supply ventilation to the compartment, while vents numbered 3 provide fresh cool air to the air filters to enable full power to be developed.

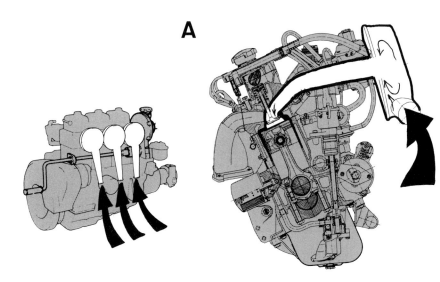

A

The sketches above and right show how much care is taken to provide good air flow to the cylinders.

Above: each cylinder has a separate air filter. Right is a large filter, while the air channel has the largest possible cross-section area and is designed to offer minimum resistance. These are the features which promote good fresh air flow. The intake and exhaust passages are so designed that the waves of air and exhaust gases in the passages help to force as much fresh air into the cylinders as possible and, simultaneously, to sweep out the residual exhaust gases. This enables more fuel to be burnt and output rises. Skilled engine tuners can raise power output by about 30% just by improving the breathing of a normal engine. Better combustion results from the increase in the fresh air and fuel mixture (petrol) or fresh air (diesel oil), and both bmep and power output increase.

Naturally no advice can be given here on tuning racing engines but if the yard has installed an engine without adequately checking the ventilation ducts breathing can be improved by removing some obstruction from the inlet duct.

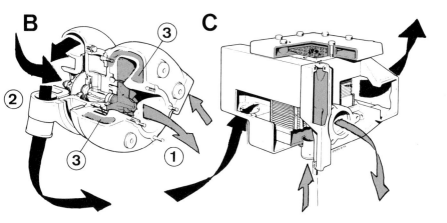

The engine will then receive more air and output will rise.

The amount of air needed purely for combustion purposes is not particularly large, but that is not the only requirement for air. Ventilation is also needed to extract the warmth arising from convection and radiation if engine room temperature is to be prevented from rising so much that power output would fall. The amount of air required is about five times as much as that needed for combustion purposes:

$$\text{Combustion air } (m^3/min) \quad = \quad \frac{\text{engine capacity } (cm^3) \times \text{rev/min}}{2,000,000}$$

A good instruction manual should state the amount of combustion air required, and more besides; the manufacturer should also give the cross-section of the fresh air ducts needed to supply combustion air and to dissipate convected and radiated heat. It is a fact that when engine compartment temperature reaches 50°C output will be about 15% lower than rating B output at the DIN 6270 standard temperature of 20°C. Output can be increased enormously by using a turbo-charger (B), the turbines being driven by the exhaust gases (1) grey arrows which in turn drive an air compressor that forces air into the cylinders (2) black arrows with the result that thermal efficiency increases and more fuel is burned.

The Volvo turbo-charger illustrated above also has a water jacket (3) to reduce the air temperature. So does the aftercooler (C); here the compressed air is cooled by water and this leads to an increase in power output. This is the reason why the specific power output of modern diesel engines matches that of petrol engines made in the sixties.

Perkins, Mercedes, MTU, Deutz and other well-known engine manufacturers have similarly increased output, but Volvo leads the field with almost 30 kW specific power output. Such a high performance unit is expensive of course, and it is a pity if faulty installation by the yard causes a drop in pressure because reduced air density affects a sensitive engine with turbo-compressor and leads to a loss of power or to exhaust smoke.

boat engines

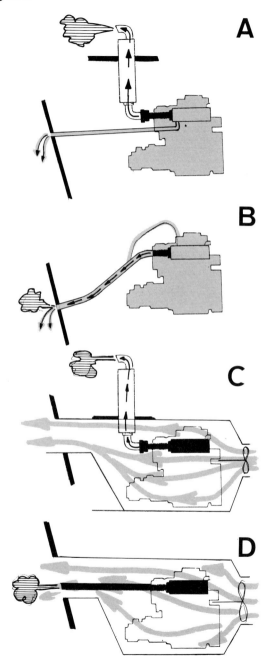

Left

The exhaust manifold normally used for a vehicle engine would become red hot in a boat's engine compartment and, as well as the danger of fire and explosion, a glowing piece of metal in the engine compartment would cause the temperature to rise so much that synthetic materials and rubber, such as cables and engine mountings, would soon be damaged, quite apart from power being reduced. There are two ways of avoiding overheating water-cooled engines: A, dry exhaust and B, wet exhaust.

The dry exhaust is the only sensible system for air-cooled engines. This is either insulated, C, or led direct to the exhaust outlet, D.

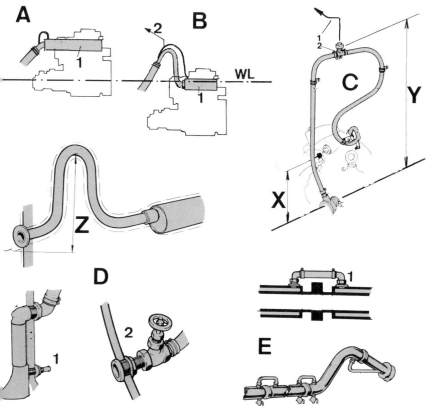

The most usual system is the wet exhaust. When water has been sprayed on to the exhaust gases the temperature drops to under 100°C and they can then be led away in hoses.

Sketch A: Above: If the engine is mounted high enough above the waterline (WL) the cooling water can be injected just beyond the water-cooled exhaust manifold (1).

boat engines

Sketch B: If the engine is below the WL a water-lock system (2) has to be used to ensure that no water can run back; it would flow through an open exhaust valve into the cylinder, on into the crankcase and through the oil strainer, not only making the engine unusable but also sinking the vessel. This can also occur if the water pump impeller is not watertight. The pipe has to loop up high to prevent the water siphoning back. 1 = exhaust manifold. 2 = water-lock.

Sketch C: A water-lock system is required if the distance (X) between the waterline and the exhaust manifold flange is less than 250 mm. The vacuum valve (1) and T-piece (2) should be at least 400–600 mm above the WL (Y).

Sketch D: another bend has to be incorporated just inboard of the exhaust outlet to prevent sea water entering. The height, Z, should be at least 350 mm. 1 = motor boat boot which exhausts below the WL. 2 = exhaust outlet with screw-down sea-cock for motor sailers and sailing boats; to be closed when the engine is not running.

Sketch E: dry exhaust with water jacket. Very costly (see cross-section 1 p. 95). Naturally a water collector and silencer are also required for a wet exhaust system.

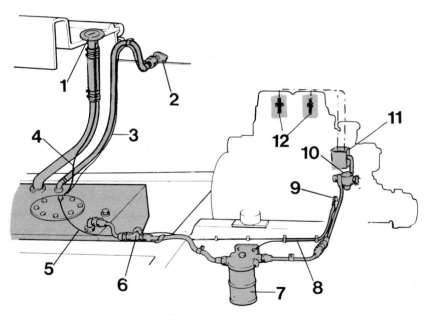

The fuel system is essentially the same for all boats between the filler cap and the fuel feed pump. The main parts are: 1 = filler cap. 2 = breather, preferably with a flame eliminator. 3, 4, 5 = earths. 6 = shut-off cock, should be close by the tank. 7 = water separator, very important. 8 = earth, leading to earth terminal (9). 10 = fuel feed pump. 11 = fuel injection pump in a diesel or carburettor in a petrol engine. 12 = injectors for diesel engines, sparking plugs for petrol engines.

Depending on the unit: leak-off pipes between fuel feed and injection pumps, step filters or fine filters, two fuel tanks, two water separators and filters, exchangeable.

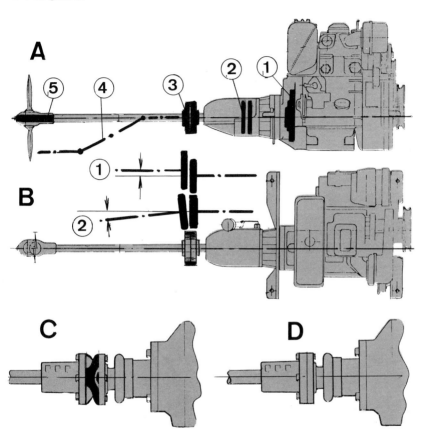

Above A: The engine's power is delivered to the propeller through a number of couplings. 1 = torsion damper between engine and gearbox. 2 = clutch which is engaged and disengaged. 3 = coupling between gearbox output shaft and propeller shaft. 4 = articulated shaft used, for example, when the angle has to be altered. 5 = shaft to propeller, using cone and spring or keyed shaft.

The engine is connected to the propeller shaft at coupling 3, and alignment must be absolutely accurate if the installation is to run faultlessly. Two checks are required:

Sketch B: checking alignment. The output shaft and the propeller shaft must be centred exactly and not be off centre as shown at 1. These shafts must also run in a straight line and not at an angle to each other. According to the degree of

boat engines

accuracy, these checks are made with a feeler gauge or a dial gauge. It is important to check both horizontally and vertically.

Sketch C shows a flexible coupling and sketch D a rigid coupling. One or other may be used, depending on the shaft layout and mountings.

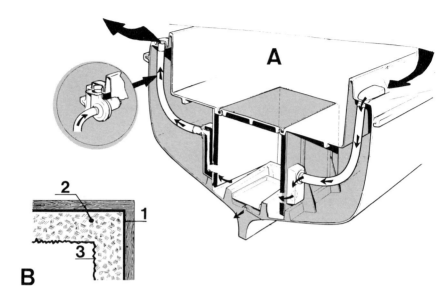

Section through a displacement hull at the engine compartment. The designer is primarily responsible for good sound-proofing of the engine compartment, the aim being to absorb sound from the air. Engine vibration is largely absorbed by the flexible engine mountings. Insulation materials vary considerably in quality, and three layers are generally used. The first essential, if noise is to be reduced, is to seal the engine compartment, making it air-tight if possible. Because the compartment has to be ventilated and the engine requires combustion air there is no alternative to leaving openings for this air to enter and, if the engine compartment temperature is to be kept within reasonalbe limits, these openings must be relatively large (see right). How effectively the noise problem is solved depends on the degree of comfort desired by the owner for whom the yard is catering.

Section B shows typical engine compartment construction.

1 = thick sound-insulating sheeting to damp sound vibration. 2 = foam lining to absorb sound. 3 = because the area of the sound-absorption material should be as large as possible material with an uneven surface is used. The sound-proofing materials employed should at least be flameproof. Completely non-inflammable materials are safer and the pores should be sealed to prevent absorption of moisture and oil. (Such materials are expensive.)

The air intake and outlet openings are sources of noise which are not easy to deal with. On the one hand they should be as large as possible to keep the engine compartment temperature low, but on the other hand a lot of noise comes out of large openings. Some alternative methods of reducing noise are shown here. 1 = an elbow in a duct offers the same resistance to intake as a metre of pipe. 2 = cowl ventilators have a greater intake diameter so that resistance is reduced. 3 = a vent protected from spray is a good solution. If an insect screen (a) is fitted the effective intake area is halved, but this is unimportant provided the area is adequate in the first place. In 4 a simple air screen (a) ahead of a sound trap serves to divert spray. A curved insect screen (b) can be added behind it and this increases the effective area. c = interior baffles to which sound-absorption material is glued. 5 = very expensive, but very efficient, is a ventilator with expansion chamber (a), pierced tubing (b) and a sound absorption layer (c). Spray drains into the bilges through d. 6 = mushroom type ventilator. This is the most effective shape. The walls are covered with sound-insulating material and absorb noise.

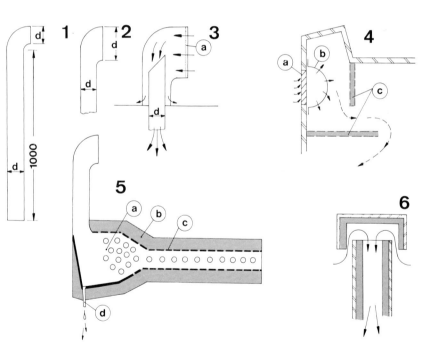

boat engines

The electrical requirements of every boat can be divided into two sections, although they have been separated all too rarely until now.

- Engine requirements (lower part of the figure right). These include the starter battery (BS), the starter (S), the ignition key (I) and the alternator (A) or dynamo. The circuit is simple. From the battery's positive terminal, via the main switch to starter terminal 30, and on to B+ on the alternator. The ignition key starts the engine by making a connection with starter terminal 50. In its first position the ignition key connects the charging indicator (a), the oil pressure light (b), the temperature gauge or light and any other monitoring instruments (c) as well as the ignition system of a petrol engine. A switch connects the extra equipment (E). Many diesel engines have a separate starting button, and indirect injecting engines often use glow plugs.

  The weak point of such an installation is the connection for extra equipment (E) because the battery can be discharged to such an extent that no voltage is left to start the engine (safety hazard). This wiring system is therefore practicable only for small sailing boats that use electricity just for navigation lights and monitoring instruments. As soon as appliances are added to increase comfort on board two separate wiring systems should be used and not, as so often recommended, a second battery in parallel. Safety is then increased because there is always adequate current for engine requirements, extra equipment being powered by the separate appliances battery (BE). A charging distributor is fitted (CD) so that both batteries can be charged by one alternator in spite of their being used for independent circuits. The electric circuit is then interrupted between X–X and the alternator current regulator is connected to terminal 61 (CD).

- The extra equipment wiring system: two-core cable must be used, and all the negative wiring connected to the battery through the terminal board (1). The positive wiring leads from the battery via the master switch to the switchboard (2, circuit breakers or switches and fuses). Individual circuits lead to the appliances. The navigation lights (3) should not all be on one circuit as here; several circuits are preferable with, at least, stern and masthead lights separate from side lights. It depends on individual requirement for comfort as to whether an independent switch is installed for each appliance (additional sources of faults). The engine room ventilator (4) should be connected to the ignition switch, particularly when a petrol engine is installed, and a time-delay device incorporated so that the engine cannot be started before the ventilator has run for several minutes.

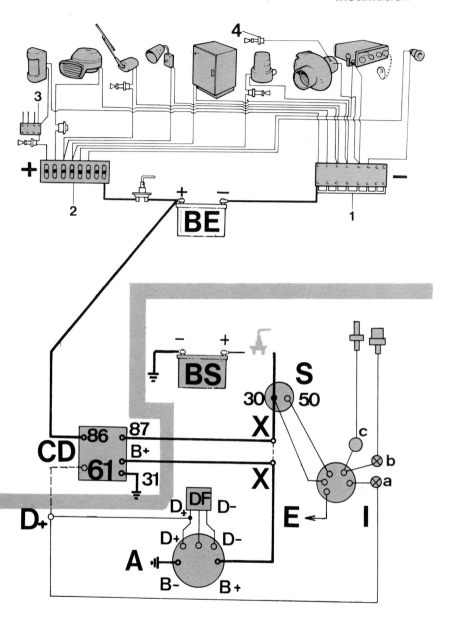

101

boat engines

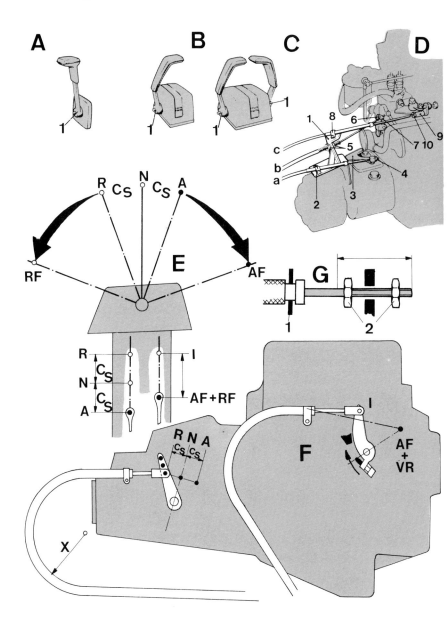

A

B

C

D

1

1

1

1

1

8   6
c   5
b   7 10 9
a
2   3   4

R C_S N C_S A

RF   E   AF

G

1   2

R   I
C_S
N
C_S
A   AF+RF

R N A
C_S C_S

F

I

AF
+
VR

X

Engine speed and gear controls. There are many different control systems, of course, but as single lever control is the most convenient it is shown here in detail. A = single lever for side mounting. B = single lever for top mounting. C = top mounting for twin engines. If the button (1) is pushed in and the lever moved forward engine speed can be altered without gear being engaged. Normally two cables are connected to the lever. In sketch D: a = gear shift push-pull cable. b = cable to operate the stop control of a diesel or the choke of a petrol engine. This, however, is usually operated independently of the single lever. c = engine speed control cable (petrol, throttle adjustment: diesel, rod controlling amount of fuel delivered). The individual parts are : 1 = bracket for cable casing. 2 = clamp for the gear cable. 3 = gear-shift arm. 4 = locknut, fine adjustment to gear-shift cable. 5 = nuts, fine adjustment to stop control cable. 6 = stop arm connecting bush. 7 = locking screw, stop control. 8 = engine speed cable clamp. 9 = ball joint of governor arm. 10 = locknut for adjustment. Sketch E shows the various lever positions: N = neutral, gear disengaged, engine ticking over. CS = clutch engaged and engine speed increased. A = ahead, AF = full ahead. R = astern. RF = full astern. The two cables react simultaneously to the movement of the lever as can be seen below the unit, and the lettering matches that above. Whereas the gear cable moves in a straight line from astern to neutral and on to ahead the engine speed cable moves only between idling speed (I) and full speed, regardless of which way the propeller is turning. This is due to a cam in the lever unit.

The effect at the engine is shown at sketch F with the gear lever in the reverse position. It has to be moved through neutral to forward gear. The engine speed control is at idling speed and is pushed forward gradually to the full speed position. As can be seen below left the cable can only be bent to a certain radius (X) before the force required to move it increases excessively and may even cause it to break. The correct leads for the cables are adjusted at the engine, gearbox and control lever.

Sketch G shows how a push-pull cable can be adjusted in greater detail. The casing is anchored at 1, and the cable itself is adjusted by means of two nuts (2). Sensitive finger tips are needed for this, and the adjusting nuts should not be fiddled about with too much unless this is unavoidable. If the engine and controls are bought separately check that either the engine manufacturer or the control supplier guarantees that no extras are required for adaptation because this can be very costly.

boat engines

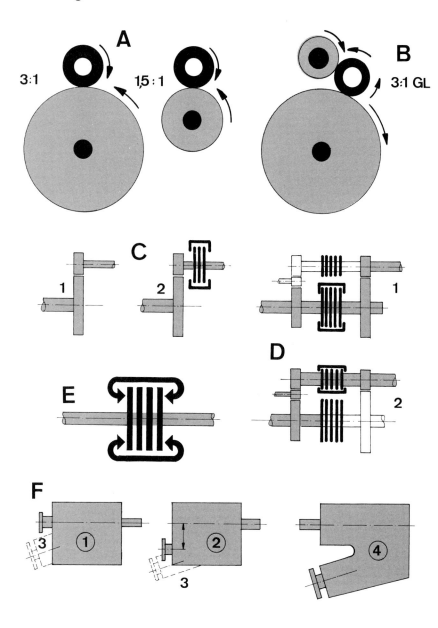

104

Reverse and reduction gear.
Sketch A: A = propeller revolutions can be reduced or increased in proportion to engine revolutions by using gear wheels with different numbers of teeth, and these will match the ratio of the diameters. For example, if the engine output gear has 17 teeth and a reduction of 3:1 is required the reduction gear must have 3 × 17 or 51 teeth. The propeller will then only revolve once while the engine revolves three times (e.g. 3,000:1,000). Some strange reduction ratio figures occur when, say, the drive gear has 48 teeth instead of 51 (2·82:1). The faster the boat the smaller can the reduction ratio be and, as the size of the gearbox is very considerably influenced by the reduction ratio, reductions of 1:2 or 1:3 are general. The propeller shaft may rotate in the same direction as, or the opposite direction to the engine output shaft, and is described as 'as engine' or 'opposite to engine'.
Sketch B: 'As engine': an intermediary gear which reverses the direction is included when both shafts are required to revolve in the same direction.
Sketch C: Reduction gear: 1 = without clutch, e.g. for small outboards which can be turned through 360°. 2 = with clutch, as generally used for small outboards and with variable pitch propellers.
Sketch D: reverse-reduction gear with two clutches. 1 is engaged for ahead and 2 for astern.
Sketch E: According to gearbox quality a dog clutch, cone clutch or multiple disc clutch may be used. They may be engaged mechanically, hydraulically or electrically depending on the type and size of the gearbox.
Sketch F: gearboxes can be fitted without (1) or with (2) offset propeller shaft, with down-angle (3) or vee drive (4) and with or without an integral thrust bearing according to which is suitable for the installation. Efficiency is largely dictated by the quality of the toothing and should be no lower than 0·94 so that the flywheel output is not reduced by more than 6%.

3. Which transmission system for which boat?

Various transmission systems for boats have been developed over the years and some are excellent for certain types of boats but virtually unusable in other types. Broadly speaking two varieties of combustion engines drive 98% of the boats world-wide that are equipped with engines:

Outboard engines are very compact and only require to be clamped to the transom. Their enormous advantage is that they are portable and can be removed; they are therefore very easy to service. Power output is high but space requirement is small, and the power to weight ratio is low. They are cheaper to buy than inboard engines, and there are no installation or maintenance problems. Stowage space required on board is minimal. The disadvantages are that weight is concentrated right aft and that fuel consumption is high because they are two-stroke engines (over 99% of all outboards are two-strokes). They are said to be less reliable than inboard engines, but that can only be attributed to improper use and poor servicing (Ch. 5). Today outboards up to 60 kW power about 95% of motor boats, and about 50% of light sailing boats up to 800 kg (1,760 lbs). The proportion is increasing.

Fixed engines are normally called inboard engines as opposed to outboards. Specific fuel consumption is lower because they are four-strokes. To be precise they are fitted in all powered boats that do not have outboards, and differ from each other largely in the way power is transmitted. They can be sub-divided as follows:

Shaft drive: conventional straight shafting or vee drive.

Outdrive, with the underwater drive unit connected directly to the engine. Alternatively called Z-drive, which reflects the course of the transmission, or inboard-outboard.

Water Jet Propulsion: the engine shaft runs in a duct and, instead of turning a propeller, drives a pump which thrusts the boat forward by forcing the water aft.

Hydrostatic Transmission: the engine pumps oil through flexible lines to drive components at the propeller.

Special Systems:
Rotary engine and propeller
Air screw and piston engine
Air screw and turbine
Propeller and turbine
Jet propulsion and
Rocket propulsion
are found only in special types of boats, partly because of their respective

disadvantages, and partly due to the state of their development. They power less than 1% of all boats and are therefore not covered here.

When evaluating the different power units today both the purchase price of the engine and the cost of installation must be taken into account because hourly wages are so high that expenditure spirals. You can easily see from the summary on the next two pages which is the most popular unit for a particular type of boat. The different varieties of power unit will then be considered more fully. The amount of power required for your boat is considered in Chapter 4, Correct handling.

Shaft drive: straight and vee drive

The normal method of transmitting power to the propeller is by a propeller shaft through the stern tube. This could be described as traditional transmission, but this immediately makes it sound rather dated. If we just consider transmission systems in relation to the length of the boat and power output, ignoring the actual numbers being used, it then appears as in the graph over that, in the power range up to 60 kW, outboards have not only displaced the conventional straight shaft layout but also the four-stroke engine. Above 60 kW outdrives predominate up to 2×200 kW. The conventional shafting system is still dominant where output is greater and is used in all intermediary types of boat where an outdrive is unsuitable. The main problems are making the stern tube watertight (a hole in the underwater body is inevitable), the high cost of installation, fitting the various circuits and aligning the engine and shaft. This in particular must not be hurried because poor alignment causes premature damage to bearings.

A further disadvantage of straight shaft and vee drive is that, when the propeller has to be changed or a check made, the boat cannot be driven on to the beach whereas the power unit of a boat with an outboard or outdrive only has to be tilted up.

Vee drive is similar to ordinary shaft drive, but the engine can be sited differently and a reduction gear or, in some cases, step-up gear fitted as well as the reverse gear.

Most of the propellers used have fixed blades and in consequence it is necessary to fit reverse gear which also reduces the revolution rate as is generally essential. A comparison with outdrives will be found on p. 115.

The details are considered in the sketches which follow.

Outdrives

Outdrives are the outcome of persistent, and not always simple development. These were produced by Volvo originally and were used first in 1956. They are also called Z-drives, reflecting the Z-shaped course of the transmission, and inboard-outboard, half their features being those of an outboard while the remainder are those of an inboard engine. Outdrives resulted from the dilemma as to where to position large engines in small boats. The stern offered itself and at the same time made it possible to design a power unit that could be tilted so that, as with an outboard, the boat could easily be run on to the beach or a trailer to check the transmission or to change the propeller. The advantages were obvious, and only technical problems had to be solved. Two sets of bevel gears

boat engines

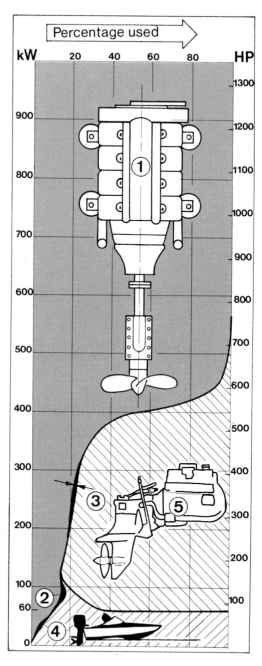

transmission systems

The graph shows the percentage of the various transmission systems for power units up to 1,000 kW, disregarding the actual number of units in use:

1. Above 500 kW (2 × 250 kW) shaft transmission alone is used, whether straight shafting or vee drive. Between about 60 kW and 500 kW outdrives predominate while below 60 kW the outboard engine is most common.
2. This bulge indicates that, at this range, the almost linear increase in shafted power units is somewhat augmented at higher output by motor sailers.
3. This section indicates jet propulsion but the proportion amounts to well under 1%.
4. Proportion of sail-drives, sales of which are increasing due to ease of installation. By comparison with the enormous number of outboard motors the proportion is obviously very small.
5. Indicates that outdrives dominate the 60–500 kW range.

It should be clear from this table that shaft drive, however traditional, is really the only practicable transmission system when power output exceeds 1 × 250 or 2 × 250 kW.

Over: main components of a simple shaft layout with only one bearing and a flexible stuffing box.

Sketch A: 1 = stern tube which passes through the hull. 2 = shaft carried in the stern tube. 3 = coupling flange, the actual type of coupling used depends on the shaft layout. 4 = stuffing box, shown in detail in sketch C. 5 = shaft bearing, made either of plastics or babbit metal according to the shaft layout (plastics are preferable). 6 = propeller with self-locking nut; there should be 5–10 mm play between propeller and stern tube. 7 = lubrication for bearing (5); water is used for plastics and grease for babbit metal bearings.

Sketch B: the three drawings show the normal methods of fitting the stern tube in boats made of GRP (laminated in), wood (screwed), steel (welded). 1 = stern tube. 2 = shaft.

Sketch C: details of a stern tube with flexible stuffing box. 1 = stuffing box. 2 = stuffing box gland. 3 = adjusting nut and locknut. 4 = six layers of packing. 5 = flexible tube connecting the stuffing box to the stern tube. 6 = hose clip; only one is shown here, there would be two. 7 = maintenance-free synthetic bushings to centre the stuffing box, thus protecting the packing from the vibration of the flexibly mounted engine.

boat engines

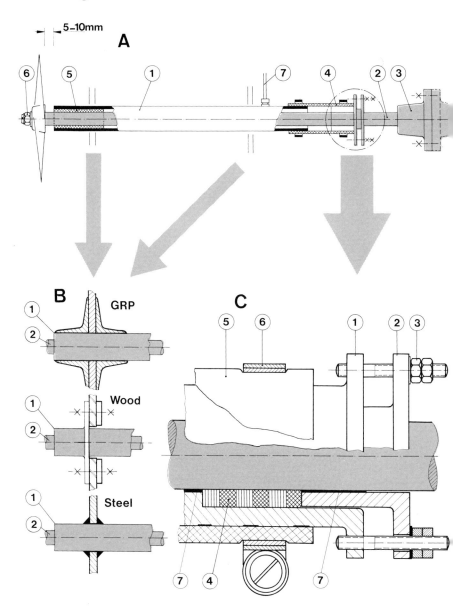

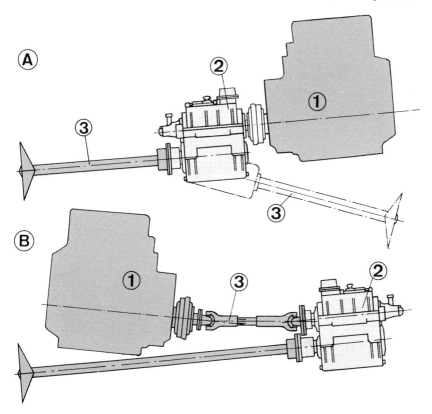

Main methods of installing an engine with shaft drive:
A = conventional shafting. 1 = engine. 2 = gearbox. 3 = shaft layout. The
dash-dotted line indicates vee drive.
B: Vee drive with articulated shaft. 1 = engine. 2 = vee drive gearbox. 3 =
articulated shaft.

Over: Transmission layouts with flexibly mounted engines. In all sketches 1 =
engine and 2 = gearbox.
A: flexibly mounted engine: gearbox with integral thrust block. 3 = flexible
   stuffing box at the stern tube.
B: where a flexibly mounted engine has an articulated shaft (3) two shaft
   bearings are required.

111

boat engines

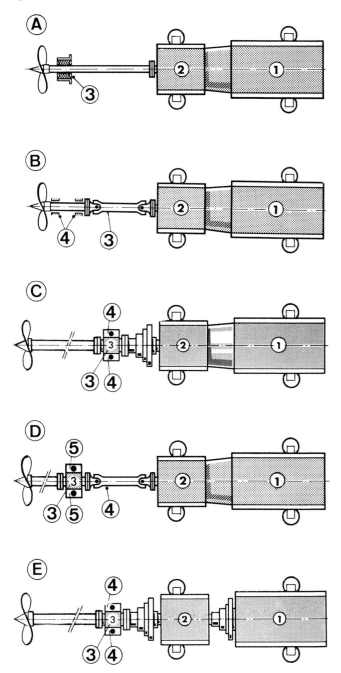

transmission systems

C: a flexibly mounted engine with a separate thrust block (3) which must be bolted firmly to the hull because it takes the thrust forces of the propeller shaft.

D: flexibly mounted engine with articulated shaft (4) and separate thrust block (3). 5 = thrust block bolts.

E: flexibly mounted engine with independently mounted gearbox (2) and separate thrust block (3). 4 = thrust block bolts.

are used to turn the drive shaft through two right angles, and they also gear down the engine revolutions so that the propeller rotates at an efficient speed.

The main difficulty was that the underwater components had to be not too clumsy if efficiency was to be higher than that of a propeller shaft with bracket. At the same time relatively great propeller diameter combined with keeping propeller rotational speed low led to high torque (torque=output × constant: revolutions) and, consequently, to greater gear tooth loading.

All these problems have been so well resolved that the underwater parts of the unit and the Z-shaped shafting are just as efficient as normal shafting, obviously complete with reverse gear. Propeller diameters have increased, underwater parts are better streamlined and, now that a rather larger fin has been added, the rudder has become more effective at lower speeds.

The greatest advantage over a shaft layout is that the outdrive is installed through a single hole in the transom which both reduces installation time (=money) and avoids many possible sources of installation faults, such as alignment. Because cooling water is drawn in through the underwater casing of the outdrive and dispatched with the exhaust gases no exhaust cooling water lines etc have to be fitted and only the fuel has to be connected.

When the power output required is higher than that of outboards, and in the motor boat range that is from 60 kW upwards, the outdrive is obviously the logical transmission system to use and it completely dominates the market. The advantages for the owner of a pleasure craft have already been stated.

The difference between the initial cost of an inboard engine with reverse gear and that of an outdrive including engine (no shaft, exhaust lines etc) is so small, amounting to 5–15%, that no buyer should find it difficult to succumb to the obvious superiority of this transmission system. In hard commercial use different problems arise (see Schottel), but these do not affect a pleasure craft because it is used for much shorter periods. You will find a comparison between normal shaft drive and outdrive on the next page.

The way the outdrive works and technical details are discussed in the sketches which follow.

The sail-drive is very similar to the outdrive but is not mounted right aft. It has been designed for sailing boats with the underwater section protruding through the bottom of the hull. I believe it will become as important as the outdrive in the next few years and I therefore consider it separately on p. 119.

boat engines

VOLVO TMD 40		VOLVO AQD 40	
Rating B	96 kW	Rating B	96 kW
Rev/min	3,600	Rev/min	3,600
No. of cylinders	6 in-line	No. of cylinders	6 in-line
Swept volume	3·59 dm³	Swept volume	3·59 dm³
Weight (with gearbox but no shaft)	from 440 kg	Weight (including transmission)	465 kg

Main installation work
Volvo TMD 40 and shaft
shaft installation
Cooling system
Exhaust system
Engine speed control
Shaft and stern tube
Propeller
Fit gear shift control
Estimated time   50 hrs

Main installation work
Volvo AQD 40/280 (outdrive)

Establish height of installation
Saw out hole in transom
Fit forward mounting
Instal engine, fit Aquamatic
Fit gear and engine speed controls

Estimated time   25 hrs

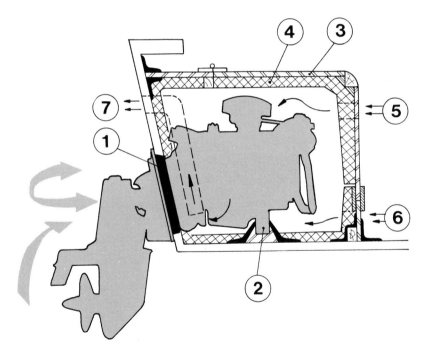

Layout of a power unit with outdrive.
Engine and transmission are delivered as a single unit. The advantages are obvious. Installation is much quicker, only one hole is made in the boat, no rudder is needed and the boat can be run on to the shore because the transmission can be tilted for inspection or to change the propeller. 1 = opening

transmission systems

in transom. 2 = cradle for flexible mounting. 3 = engine compartment casing. 4 = sound insulation. 5 = combustion air. 6 = air for engine compartment ventilation. 7 = engine compartment air outlet.

When an engine with outdrive is compared to an engine with conventional shafting the enormous advantages of installing the outdrive can be seen. Fitting the shafted layout can take roughly twice as long. An outdrive of this size might take about 25 hours to install compared to about 50 hours for normal shafting, but these are the times it would take skilled workers who know exactly where each part goes. A further prerequisite for keeping to such a schedule is that the yard must have prepared the boat to receive the unit. The time taken increases considerably if an engine bed still has to be laminated in, or if difficulties arise over fitting ventilators, the exhaust system, or some sea-cocks.

A further advantage of making this comparison is that some idea is gained of what parts are needed apart from the engine itself.

To go through the list: the fuel system with water separator and accessories has to be fitted in both cases. The cooling system is required only with shaft installation because coolant is sucked in through the outdrive trunk and flows out with the exhaust. Both require an electrical system, controls, engine mountings, bilge pumps and instruments. The extra cost of the shaft layout is therefore comparable to the higher initial price of the outdrive. In the table below the major jobs are listed again, with the times required for fitting, and this shows that, although purchase price is much the same, double the time is required for installing the shaft layout, and for power units of this output this amounts to about 10% of the purchase price.

	TMD40	AQD40
Price of the engine in 1978, with gearbox or outdrive	4,998	5,616
Fuel system, including filter with water separator and connections, fuel lines etc	90	90
Cooling system, intake, hosing etc	35	—
Exhaust system, tubing, water-cooled silencer etc	175	—
Electrical system, charging distributor, hour meter etc	100	100
Flexible mountings	50	75
Bilge pump	20	20
Engine controls, instrument panel, push-pull cables control lever etc	200	200
Shaft installation, steel shaft, zinc nut, stern tube, stuffing box, lubrication etc	250	—
Propeller	75	75
	5,993	6,176

OR

Price of the engine in 1978, with gearbox or outdrive	4,998	5,616

115

boat engines

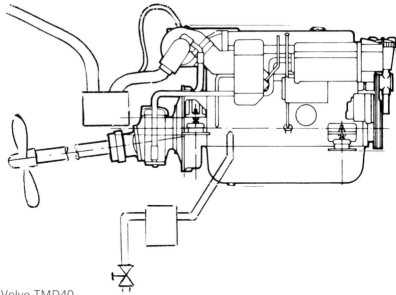

Volvo TMD40

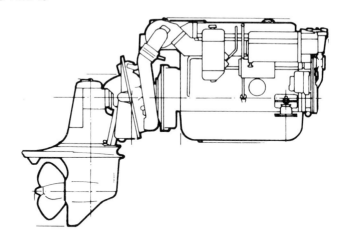

Volvo AQD40

Fuel system, including filter with water separator and connections, fuel lines etc	+1·8%	+1·6%
Cooling system, intake, hosing etc	+0·7%	+ –
Exhaust system, tubing, water-cooled silencer etc	+3·5%	+ —
Electrical system, charging distributor, hour meter etc	+2%	+1·8%
Flexible mountings	+1%	+1·3%

Bilge pump	+0·4%	+0·4%
Engine controls, instrument panel, push-pull cables		
control lever etc	+4%	+3·6%
Shaft installation, steel shaft, zinc nut, stern tube,		
stuffing box, lubrication etc	+5%	+ —
Propeller	+1·5%	+1·3%

Although the outdrive costs roughly 11% more than the inboard engine by the time the extra fittings needed have been bought the outdrive is only about 3% more expensive.

Check list for price comparison of Shaft   Z-drive

Price of engine and gearbox or outdrive
Fuel system
Filter with water separator and connections
Tank cover
Feed line, connections, fuel lines
Fuel lines
Cooling system
Cooling water intake
Hosing
Exhaust system
Exhaust hose
Water-cooled silencer
Electrical system and instruments
12 v. charging distributor
24 v. for two battery system
Hour meter
Extension cable
Instruments 2·5 m
Main switch
Flexible engine mountings
Bilge pump
Gear change and engine speed controls
Push-pull cable for engine speed
Gear change
Push-pull cable for gear change
Propeller installation
Propeller shaft (steel)
Zinc nut
Stern tube
Stuffing box
Lubrication fittings
Hose
Propeller (varying sizes)

boat engines

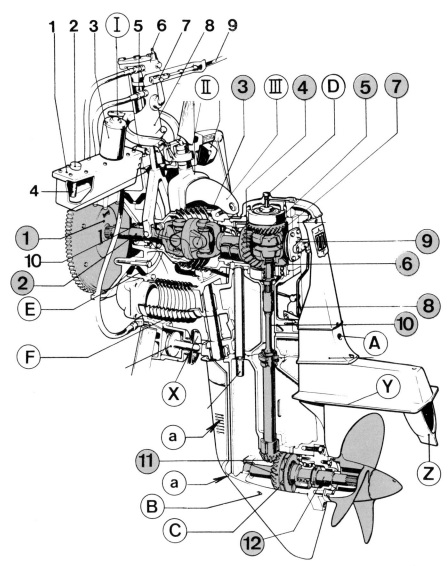

Outdrive components, using the Volvo Aquamatic 270T as an example. The transmission is shaded grey, and the numbers in the grey circles should be followed. Flywheel (1) with torsion damper; this is virtually the start of the outdrive. The drive shaft (2) is splined into the torsion damper and transmits engine output to the universal joint (3) which, alone, is responsible for the great benefits of the outdrive (trimming, tilting, steering). Then comes the first bevel gear (4) where gear is selected, either the upper (5) or lower (6) gear being engaged for ahead and astern drive depending on which way the engine rotates. Gear is engaged by means of the cone clutch (7), the gear shift link rod (8) and the shift mechanism (9). The vertical shaft (10) transmits the power to the second bevel gear (11) where the direction is changed to drive the horizontal propeller shaft (12).

The steering components are the steering lever (I), the steering arm (II) and the housing round the universal joint (III).

The unit shown here has a hydraulic tilting system which is labelled with black numbers, 1–10. 1 = hydraulic reservoir. 2 = filler cap. 3 = hydraulic pump motor. 4 = hydraulic oil filter; hydraulic controls are badly affected by dirt. 5 = tilting piston. 6 = air bleed. 7 = control lever. 8 = raising cylinder. 9 = control cable. 10 = lifting arms.

There is a hydraulic system (X) for altering trim as well as the hydraulic tilting arrangement. This acts like trim tabs and enables the outdrive to be adjusted to the boat's longitudinal axis.

The cooling water inlet is at (a-a), while the outlet lies with the exhaust in the fin (Z) beneath the cavitation plate (Y). The fin also serves to counter sideways propeller thrust.

Oil for the outdrive is poured in at the screw (A) and drained at B. The oil is circulated by pump C and the level checked by the dipstick (D).

The hole through the transom is made watertight by the rubber diaphragm (E), while the exhaust gases pass through rubber bellows (F) and into the trunk to be exhausted at Z.

Sail-drive

Sail-drive, sometimes abbreviated to S-drive, is merely an outdrive with folding propeller driven by an engine of between 5–30 kW output. With one exception these are diesel engines. This transmission system, which was developed by Volvo and OMC, is a logical progression from the outdrive for use in sailing boats.

The aim is to make installation in series-production craft as simple and fault-free as possible. Sail-drives are delivered complete with a cradle which is then matched to the hull and laminated in with GRP. The fuel has to be connected, the exhaust system installed, control cables fitted to the gear and engine speed control lever, and the unit is then ready for use.

Conservatively-minded people, of course, must first overcome some misgivings, but progressive yards have been fitting these power units into series production craft since 1975, and the results have confirmed their decision.

boat engines

Main components of Volvo's sail-drive.
The engine (1), transmission (2) and cradle (3) form a single unit. The flexible mountings, fitted in three places (4), and the rubber diaphragm (5) ensure that

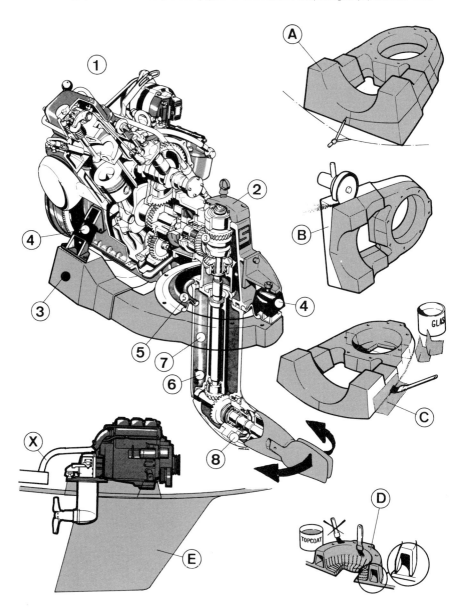

transmission systems

the unit is not attached directly to the boat. The cooling water inlet lies underwater (6). Coolant runs through the trunk (7) to the exhaust. This is the only opening in the hull apart from that for the transmission.

Two zinc rings (8) protect the propeller from corrosion, and the folding propeller offers little resistance when the boat is under sail. Installation is much simpler than that of a normal shaft layout (see p. 136 for comparison).

The cradle (A) delivered with the engine is matched to the hull shape by scribing, and part B is sawn off. The cradle now only has to be laminated into the hull (C + D).

It is to be expected that some designer will go so far as to integrate the sail-drive into the fin keel as in figure E, and this would be quite possible if two more rubber diaphragms were used.

Schottel drive

Twenty five years ago Schottel produced a transmission system which is essentially the same as the outdrive, differing only in that it is not directly connected to the engine but is driven by an articulated shaft. This means that the engine does not have to be installed right aft. Unlike normal outdrive, which at present is limited to about 250 kW, Schottel drive can be used up to about 2,500 kW. It can be fitted at the stern like the outdrive, or under the hull like the sail-drive. Although more robust and less 'yachty' it has one advantage over the two transmission systems used for yachts, outdrive and sail-drive, in that it can be turned through 360° and this means that no reverse gear is required.

Schottel drive has been used successfully for years in work boats, both for displacement boats, such as tugs, and for semi-displacement boats where large propeller diameters are general (about 700 mm to 900 mm diameter propellers at 200 kW), and where aesthetic considerations have to give way to increased manoeuvrability. In my opinion it is only a matter of time before increasing wages lead to the development of a combined outdrive, sail-drive and Schottel rudder propeller so that central engines for larger yachts can be fitted as complete units consisting of engine and transmission, with a minimum of sources of installation faults and shorter fitting time.

Hydrostatic drive

When hydrostatic drive is used the engine can be mounted well away from the propeller without the need for articulated shafts, linkages, and shaft tunnels because power is hydraulically transmitted by means of oil. The engine drives a pump which forces the fluid through flexible piping to a turbine, which in turn drives the propeller. There are a few makes on the market today, and some small single and twin-cylinder diesels are equipped with hydraulic transmission and installed in boats. The numbers are not very great because hydrostatic drive is much less efficient than shaft or sail-drive. The reduction in efficiency is about 20% but, bearing in mind the normal output of about 20 kW, this can be offset fairly cheaply by choosing a more powerful engine.

Another disadvantage, however, is cost and this is why hydrostatic transmission is generally limited to boats where difficulties arise over fitting normal shafting or sail-drive.

boat engines

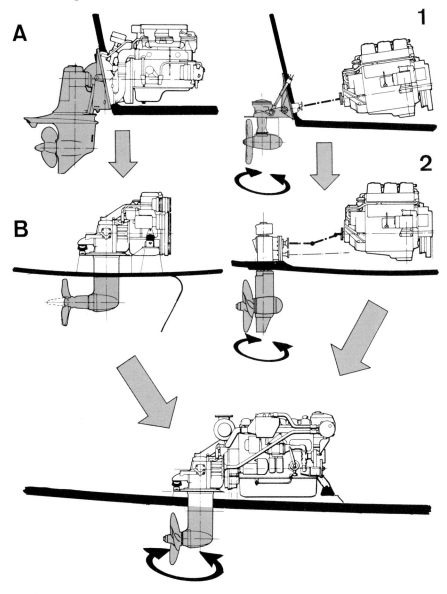

The outdrive (A) requires a reverse gear. It is highly developed and extremely suitable for fast planing boats too.
The sail-drive (B) cannot be steered and is installed under the hull of sailing

122

transmission systems

boats; power output up to about 30 kW.
1. Like the outdrive the Schottel rudder propeller can be fitted at the stern, and its advantage over the outdrive is that it can be turned through 360° which gives excellent manoeuvrability without need of reverse gear.
2. Like the sail-drive the Schottel rudder propeller can be installed beneath the hull. Advantage: it can be turned through 360° so no reverse gear is required. Manoeuvrability excellent.
Below: A possible larger transmission unit for installation in yachts with central engines. This combined transmission system would use elements of the sail-drive, outdrive and Schottel systems.

The figure shows a hydrostatic drive layout, and the example here is the Volvo MD 11. The hydraulic pump (1) is coupled to the engine and drives the hydraulic motor (2) through two pipes; there is also a return pipe. The hydraulic motor then drives the shaft and propeller. Unlike normal shaft drive the engine can be sited at the most advantageous position. Efficiency can best be compared by referring to the engine illustrated because the MD 11 is also available with reverse and reduction gear or with sail-drive. The manufacturer gives the drop in power as 26% for hydrostatic drive, 4·5% for reduction gear and 4% for sail-drive. When it comes to price hydrostatic drive is the most expensive, as already mentioned.

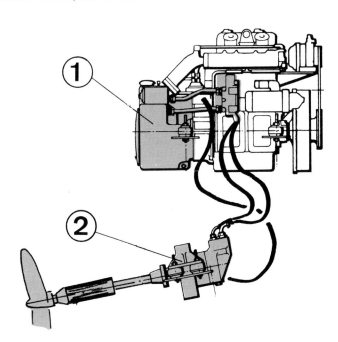

boat engines

Water jet propulsion

Some years ago just the idea of driving a jet boat enticed motor boat enthusiasts into a trial drive. Feelings have calmed down since then. The term jet propulsion sounds more exciting than the more correct definition of water jet propulsion. In some circles it is still considered regrettable that so little has come out of the jet age for motor boats. Taking similar boats, namely fast, light motor boats, water jet propulsion has three major disadvantages when compared with normal shafting, vee drive and outdrive.

- equal performance is only obtained with extremely light, and therefore expensive boats.
- when engine speed has to be reduced for some reason, such as seaway, efficiency is immediately very seriously affected
- manoeuvrability is less good at lower speeds.
  Water jet propulsion has only one advantage
- the propeller cannot be damaged in shoal waters because there is no propeller. The pump which accelerates the water is fitted inside the duct.

In our waters, in any case, the areas where water jet propulsion is advisable are rare. Power output ranges up to about 40 kW.

The figure shows the 40 kW Castoldi-Jet 1100/04. 1 = engine. 2 = pump. 3 = jet. 4 = the direction in which the water is expelled is altered by lowering a plate for astern motion.

4. Correct handling

The first step towards correct use of the engine is to provide the right amount of power for the boat, and this means that boat and engine must be matched to each other. Only when this condition is fulfilled can the engine be driven correctly for its intended purpose, namely safely, comfortably and economically.

Power matching and speed
From the point of view of 'handling the engine properly' wrong powering, as is general in about 50% of all boats, is an absurdity. Twist and turn as you will the hull form of a planing boat makes a poor displacement hull, and the many dealers who offer engines stating that they are suitable for anything from a displacement boat to a planing hull cannot therefore be justified. The case is quite different when outputs varying by ±15% are offered for a boat. Many other factors affect the decision as to how much power is required, and these can only be resolved by gathering facts. Avoid senseless overpowering which affects safety adversely; power does not result only in speed. The whole question can be far better explained by illustrations than by a spate of words.

Economy, consumption and range
The reason why people are not always sure how to use an engine economically is due to false ideas about the causes of high consumption combined with uncertainty as to what is an economical engine speed rather than to the engine's insatiable thirst. Consumption was discussed in the section on 'Power output between the fuel tank and the speedometer', but only in relation to fuel consumed by the engine relative to output near the flywheel. Although here consumption is again related to power output, boat speed and distance covered are now also involved. The specific fuel consumption of the engine in g/kWh at the relevant partial load and engine speeds remains unchanged because, although consumption in litres or gallons per hour varies from boat to boat, the characteristic way that a given engine burns fuel does not alter. The point at which to start has already been discussed in connection with the performance graph on p. 76. It is the point where the propeller blocks engine speed. This is selected by the manufacturer (rated engine speed at the appropriate maximum output). In the graphs which follow this is taken to be 100% output and 100% engine speed; in other words, the point where the propeller's requirement for power matches full load values.

125

boat engines

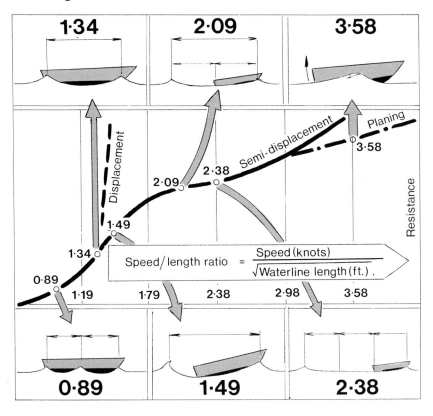

The curved line shows how resistance increases in relation to the speed to length ratio ($V/\sqrt{L}$). This is the most practical way to establish the various stages in boat speed. The relationship between the waterline length and the lengths of the waves formed by the boat is shown in the sketches. Displacement boats with round sterns do not exceed $V/\sqrt{L} = 1·49$ because resistance increases enormously as indicated by the broken line. $V/\sqrt{L} = 0·89$ requires only half the power called for at $V/\sqrt{L} = 1·34$. Above $V/\sqrt{L} = 2·98$ dynamic lift increases and partial planing occurs; these are semi-displacement boats. Only above $V/\sqrt{L} = 3·58$ can there be talk of a real planing hull and the dash-dotted curve indicates the resistance met by a planing boat. The actual moment when a boat starts to plane properly depends on how planing is defined: Marconi gives $V/\sqrt{L} = 3·98$ and Baader gives $V/\sqrt{L} = 5·96$ but I prefer Marconi's definition.

The graph enables the speed to length ratio to be determined with a given waterline length in feet or metres and at a given speed. The example entered is of a boat with a waterline length of 19·7 ft or 6 metres (LOA about 25 ft or 7·5 m). At A she makes about 4 knots and at that speed the waves formed are about half the waterline length (cf. 1 overleaf). If she were a displacement boat with a round stern she could not exceed point B (cf. 3) because the stern would be sucked into the wave trough. As a semi-displacement boat she would make about 14 knots at C, V/$\sqrt{L}$ = 2·98 (cf. 8) but a boat of this length with a planing hull would start to plane at D at speeds above about 17 knots (cf. 10).

The speed ranges to be avoided are those where the displacement/semi-displacement and semi-displacement/planing modes overlap; they are uneconomical and the boat handles poorly.

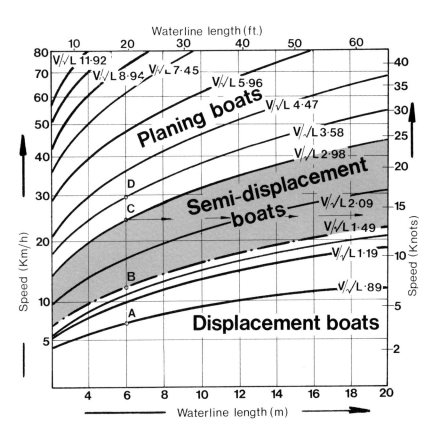

boat engines

As the boat passes from displacement to semi-displacement and planing modes her longitudinal running trim, the trim angle, changes. The bow lifts due to the formation of the waves (A–B) and the effect of the wake (B–Y). Then the stern is raised by the incidence of dynamic lift (X) and the transition to planing (C, D).

The trim angle of a displacement boat with a round stern (1–3) will increase to about 10° at maximum speed, $V/\sqrt{L} = 1\cdot49$, because the stern squats in the wave troughs as in Y. That of a flat-bottomed displacement boat, if immoderately overpowered, would increase to about 15° (Z). A good semi-displacement boat with no trim tabs will alter her trim angle as shown in the line A, B, X, C1 but an underpowered planing boat would suffer a disastrous trim angle of 8–10 (C2) at $V/\sqrt{L} = 2\cdot98$. At $V/\sqrt{L} = 3\cdot57$ a good planing boat would have a trim angle of about $3\frac{1}{2}°$. A planing boat with deep vee hull and a trim angle of about 7° could reduce the angle to about $3\frac{1}{2}°$ by fitting trim tabs. D2 = planing boats with deep veed hull. The line B, X, C1, D, could be a boat with trim tabs fitted.

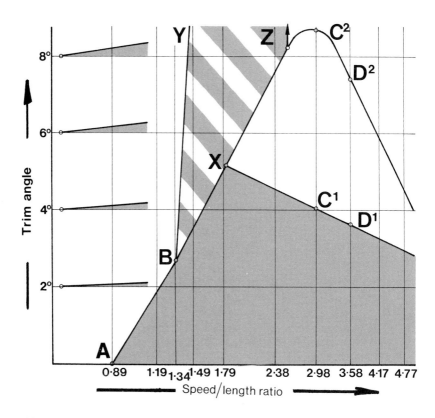

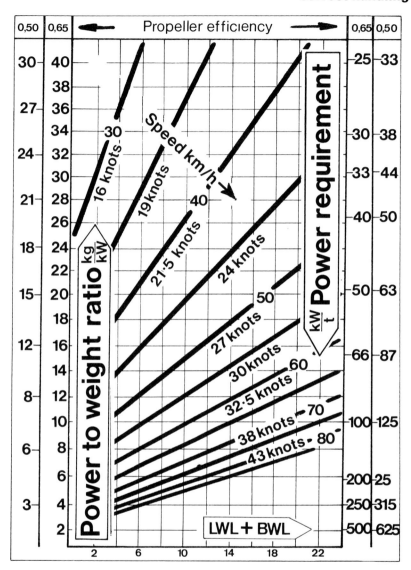

● Speed, power to weight ratio and powering of planing cruisers.
   The brake power required for a given planing boat and a particular speed can
be determined from this diagram. It can also be used to indicate the degree of
propeller efficiency of any planing boat. Marconi's figures in 'Wie konstruiert
und baut man ein Boot' have been used as a basis, power being measured at the

boat engines

gearbox output shaft with combustion air at 30°C, good sized air ducts, one shaft bearing and a stuffing box. The power to weight ratio figures on the left hand scale and the powering figures right relate to propeller efficiencies of 0·65 and 0·5. If combustion air temperature is 40°C or higher actual speed will correspond to a 10–15% reduction in brake power. Should there be more than one shaft bearing allow a reduction of about 10%. Deep veed hulls will be 10% slower.

To convert British measurements multiply feet by 0·3048, pounds by 0·4536 and horse power by 0·7457 to obtain the number of metres, kilogrammes and kilowatts. One tonne = 1,000 kg.

Thus a boat with a waterline length of 30' 6" and a waterline beam of 9' (total 12 metres), weighing 2,500 lbs (1,134 kg) with an 80 hp (60 kW) engine would have a power to weight ratio of 18·9 kg/kW and the powering would be 52·9 kW/tonne. Given propeller efficiency of 0·50 maximum speed should be about $22\frac{1}{2}$ knots but with improved propeller efficiency of 0·65 speed would be about 25 knots.

● For a displacement boat 2·5 kW brake power per tonne is required to achieve displacement speed, $V/\sqrt{L} = 1·34$, with waves as long as the LWL, when propeller efficiency is about 0·5. Given the same degree of propeller efficiency only 1·25 kW/tonne is needed for $V/\sqrt{L} = 1·2$ which is about 90% of hull speed, and for 66% of hull speed only 0·4 kW/t suffices. When using this rough guide make the same allowances as given above for planing boats.

Trial run and testing

How thoroughly a boat can be tried out before purchase depends on the atmosphere when discussing the sale, the quality of the boat, the seller's economical position and the purchase price itself. It must be emphasized that there is no substitute for a trial run, and the more thorough the better. The procedure should be as follows:

● obtain all available printed information about both boat and engine, including test reports from magazines etc. and read it all through before the trial run

● once on board go through the instruction and maintenance booklets point by point

● check the individual circuits (air, cooling, fuel etc) —see engine installation chapter

● during the trial run check particularly whether the boat is travelling as fast at the end of the trial as at the first full speed run (after at least 5 minutes warming up). If there is a small variation of 50–100 rev/min or $\frac{1}{2}$ a knot suspect poor engine compartment ventilation and confirm this by opening the hatch and rechecking the speed

● as boats are always lighter on a trial trip than later when in normal use try to take guests with you to make up the weight you will have on board later;

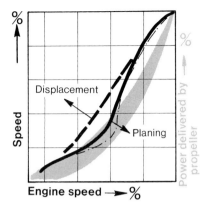

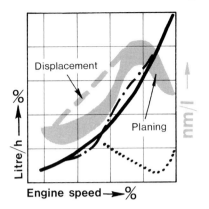

Engine speed ➤ %   Engine speed ➤ %

The graph (top left) shows the propeller's power requirement shaded grey. Planing boats lie at the lower limit of the area and displacement boats at the upper limit. Theoretically the speed curve should be similar but, in practice, it runs more like the black lines. The difference between planing boats and displacement boats (broken line) is because the former plane over the waves.

The graph (right) shows that the related fuel consumption in litres per hour is also less smooth in practice and varies greatly according to the boat and engine (e.g. like the dash-dotted line). Naturally there is another extremely important factor—how far the boat will travel on one litre (or gallon) of fuel. This is indicated by the grey curve and, again, the difference between planing and displacement boats is due to the fact that planing boats are lifted above the waves. The actual moment when the boat starts to plane will vary according to the powering, but the aim should be at about 60% of engine speed. As can be seen the greatest distance is covered at 80% engine speed and 60% consumption. The lowest dotted curve indicates the engine's specific fuel consumption. On board there is a sharp drop to the most economical range at between 90% and 80% of engine speed. Note that these curves are only characteristic of what is experienced in individual boats. Every boat is different and if the owner relies on exact data he must work out the figures for himself.

otherwise you could get a false impression of her behaviour under way
● a statement that the boat behaves as desired with a propeller different to the one fitted for the trial trip is not worth much
● as to the propeller, the general principle is that larger diameter, smaller pitch and greater reduction ratio (lowest revolutions) are preferable=see propeller efficiency
● once you have bought the boat you should try to establish consumption, speed and other figures found by experience. The following pages show how this is done.

boat engines

These are the figures that an owner needs to calculate for his boat. The graph shows three planing boats about 30 ft (9 m) in length which make about 30 knots. The small figures indicate the speed to length ratio.

Top: the longitudinal trim angle changes markedly as speed increases. There are several characteristic stages that need to be noted. 1 when the boat's stern is sucked down into the trough of the wave. 2 maximum trim angle; in planing boats this should be reached at 50% of engine speed. If later the engine is not sufficiently powerful. 3 when the stern lifts and the boat starts to plane. 4 maximum speed.

Bottom left: note boat speed at the engine speeds established above.

Bottom right: working out fuel consumption figures is both difficult and tedious. It is fairly satisfactory to use the figures from the engine's full load curve, converting them to propeller output in the same way as for specific fuel consumption. To measure them is time-consuming and complicated. The curve showing nautical miles per litre is found by dividing speed by consumption in litres (or gallons) per hour, and this enables a diagram such as that on the right to be drawn to show the range of a tankful of fuel.

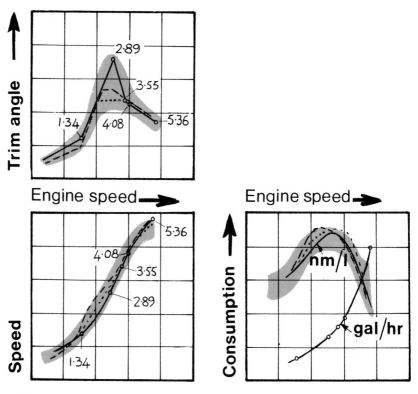

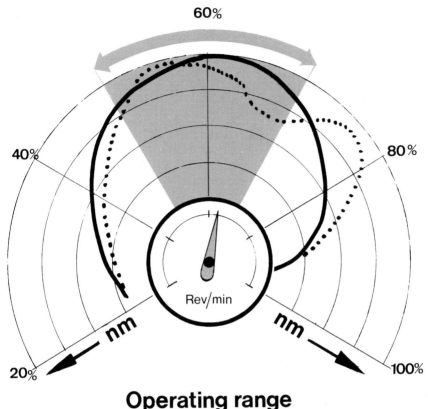

correct handling

60%

40%

80%

Rev/min

20%

100%

Operating range

Operating range. This graph showing the operating range has been drawn as a polar diagram deliberately because of the similarity to a tachometer. The figures for distance covered per gallon or litre are multiplied by the fuel tank's capacity and related to the various engine speeds. Thus the distance that can be covered at various engine speeds is always in view. Every owner should draw such a diagram for his boat, or note down the figures. Naturally this figure can also be drawn relating to boat speed.

Optimum consumption (grey) varies between 50% and 70% of engine speed according to the powering and the type of hull, and may be far from as regular as the black line here. Curves like the dotted lines are nothing unusual and, if the maxima occur at a favourable range, this is hardly disadvantageous.

133

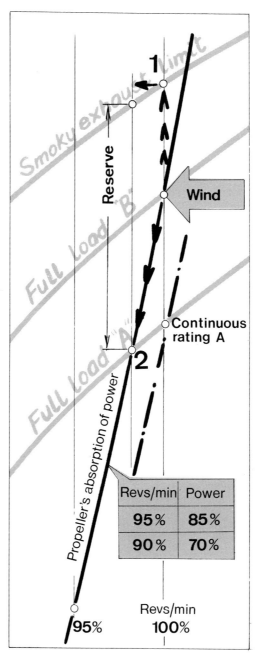

What has been stated on the previous pages is helpful when using the engine at sea, when planning voyages and when making a purchase, but there are many other factors of which one should at least be aware. The graph is a small section of that already frequently used, and shows the point where the propeller curve cuts the engine's full load curve at X. When the wind increases resistance rises and the engine has to deliver more power. This is will do as long as it is able to do so. It can increase output up to the limit when smoke is seen in the exhaust (1) but the propeller will become less efficient because of the increased loading. The boat will move more slowly, engine speed will drop, resistance will decrease and the propeller will then require far less power (2). As soon as engine speed drops the engine can again deliver more power to the propeller because the distance between the propeller curve and the smoky exhaust limit increases enormously, and this can be described as reserve power. A cruising boat will be less sensitive to wind and sea at high engine speeds if the propeller is matched to continuous rating A rather than to yacht rating B which is measured only over a short period (one hour at rated speed in a total of six hours). Engine speed can then be maintained longer and the engine used at a more favourable range, which means lower consumption and longer service life.

On page 136:
To establish whether the propeller is the correct size, load your boat as for normal use, say with two people for water-skiing. Run the engine until it is warm and then take her up to full speed. If the engine revolutions match the figure in the instruction manual the propeller pitch is correct (A). If the engine is running too fast (B) the pitch is too fine. If the engine does not run as fast as the speed specified the pitch is too coarse (C).

Altering the load on board will tell you whether the fault really lies with the propeller. If the engine was running too fast take one or more extra people on board (B1), and if the engine now runs at the correct speed the propeller was wrong. In the case of C reduce the number on board (C1). If the engine still does not run at the right speed it is the engine which is at fault.

If the propeller is correct buy a spare, but if the propeller does not give perfect results keep it in reserve.

boat engines

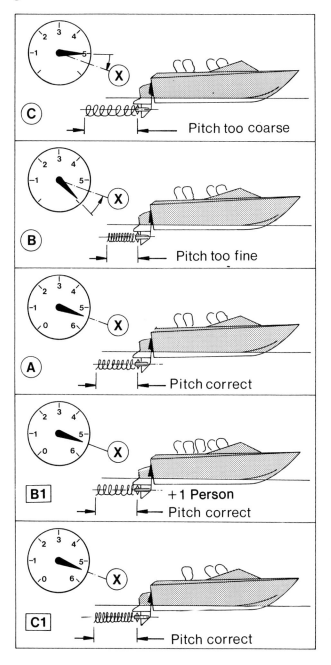

C — Pitch too coarse

B — Pitch too fine

A — Pitch correct

B1 — +1 Person — Pitch correct

C1 — Pitch correct

Handling and durability

As already stated in the paragraph on powering, a boat's behaviour under engine depends on how well boat and engine are attuned, and this is equally true of sailing boats. Manoeuvrability is greatly affected by the propeller, and a large propeller that rotates slowly makes handling easier.

The way an owner drives his boat depends largely on his character, and fortunately common sense prevails. This is most clearly shown by the fact that hardly any petrol engines are now fitted to boats of over 25 ft (8 m); diesel engines are preferred in spite of the higher initial cost. Four important points concern the engine and its length of service life:

● Maintenance should be carried out scrupulously (see chapter on maintenance and the instruction manual) and preservation from corrosion in particular. Our boat engines do not break down as a result of being used. We ruin them.

● Never run the engine at full speed before it is really warm; at the very earliest after five minutes, but 15 minutes is preferable.

● Only use 95% of engine speed which is equivalent to 80% of power and reserve the 5% for exceptional circumstances. Engines are so highly rated these days (rating B=maximum useful output) that thermal stresses are very high (see rating B).

● The reliability and durability of an engine is increased enormously if checking the most important points becomes a matter of routine (see maintenance). This means that ears, eyes and, yes, even the body must be subconsciously aware of the engine, confirming that it is not overloaded. Good skippers will even wake from a deep sleep when, for example, the wind increases slightly causing the engine to work harder, or when the noise alters in shallow waters.

On page 138:
Resistance to forward movement is due mainly to friction and hull shape. Both with planing boats and displacement boats this means that the wetted surface and depth of immersion should be kept to the minimum. The two types of resistance are so inter-related that resistance due to hull shape increases when the wetted area (planing surface) decreases. Optimum running trim therefore has to be found for each boat with a given engine. As a general rule the angle of the bottom to the water should be about 3–6°, but the exact angle can only be established by trying different trim angles. The best will be that when the boat is travelling fastest.
1. The trim angle is too great: the wetted area (grey) is small, it is true, but hull resistance is great (black wedge amidships).
2. Trim angle is correct: resistance due to shape and frictional resistance are balanced; speed is highest.
3. If the boat is too flat frictional resistance is very great and, although resistance due to shape is small, this generally also causes a reduction in speed.

boat engines

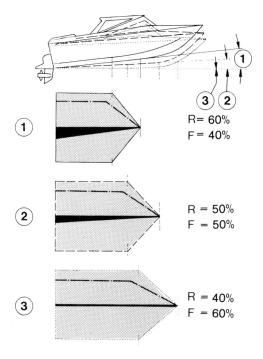

Another factor is powering. Very powerful engines would raise the boat further out of the water (dash-dotted line in 1–3), reducing both wetted surface and hull resistance. With a less powerful engine the boat would sit lower in the water and the aim would then be to increase the wetted area so as to reduce hull shape resistance.

Although the advice I am about to give involves a lot of work you and your boat will only benefit. Find an area where a distance of 100 yards can be measured (1–2) with an approach area on either side. 200 yards is preferable for boats over 30 ft in length. The actual figures obtained over this distance will be useful later. 3 and 4 are buoys or stakes which show you when the markers are abeam if you have to keep some distance offshore; when buoy and marker comes in line you can check the time accurately. Cover this stretch at varying engine speeds, checking the boat's trim angle, and note down the speeds. Establish the typical stages in speed as shown on p. 126. Turning radius and air in the propeller. To increase your sensitivity to the boat and the engine make ever tighter turns at full speed. You will notice that the boat becomes progressively slower in the turn until the point is reached when she skids sideways off course (1) or the propeller sucks in air. You cannot help but notice air in the propeller because the engine makes a loud noise and the boat slows down. For correct handling at such a moment, as soon as the propeller starts to suck air reduce engine speed until the stern drops; then increase engine speed (2). Quite a tight turn can be made if you approach point 3 at full speed, cut engine speed and put the helm hard over (4). The stern will have dropped in the meanwhile and you can then pull her into the turn with the control lever at full ahead.

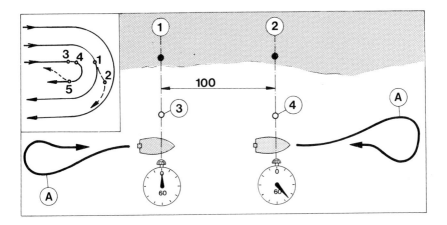

5. Maintenance and care

Engine defects, uneven running, poor starting and such matters are not bad luck. A defect or a failure, whatever it may be, generally builds up over a longer period, and this normally occurs when the engine is lying idle rather than when it is in use as is so often and wrongly assumed.

Length of service life

Diesel engines in commercial use run for 2,000 hours and more a year, and their average life is 4,000–6,000 hours. These figures are based on experience and are quoted by major engine manufacturers with thousands of engines in commercial use. It is no longer unusual for pistons and cylinder walls to survive 15,000 hours, while connecting rods and main bearings may even last for 25,000 working hours. This is proved by manufacturers' figures whose expenses in connection with guarantees have dropped some 50–70% in the last decade. Nowadays with the life of every component known exactly, related to 100% reliability, many large industrial undertakings work to a planned replacement schedule and renew all parts in good time so that interruptions are virtually excluded. Maintenance is then guaranteed by regular servicing agencies.

However we are left with the quite normal figure of 4,000 hours before an engine requires a basic overhaul, and that means new moving parts or an exchange engine. The average boat engine used as the main power unit for a motor cruiser will, at most, run for 250 hours a year and, on that basis, an engine should run for 16 years without major repairs before totalling 4,000 working hours. As an engine can have three full overhauls this means that a diesel engine built to today's standards can run for 16,000–24,000 hours before being written off. Taking the 250 hours a year, which is rarely achieved by a boat, that is the equivalent of between 64 and 96 years use. In other words, every modern commercial diesel engine converted for marine use ought to last at least as long as the vessel in which it is installed provided that it is

- well cared for
- regularly serviced and
- carefully handled

Reading figures like this naturally will not cause you to jump out of your chair in surprise; they must be put in perspective.

A new diesel engine, installed in a yacht now, would require a basic overhaul in about 1994. The second overhaul would occur in 2010 and the third in 2026.

The engine would not breathe its last until 2042. The reason that such figures are not always reached in boats is due largely to the fact that the long periods lying idle harm the engine, and the moving parts in particular.

The table below shows that a sailing boat's auxiliary engine would be 40 years old before totalling 4,000 hours. The intervals between servicing yacht engines also differ very considerably from those recommended for commercial craft.

Working hours in one year

Season 6 months	Weekends 24	Motor cruiser hours of use		Motor sailer hours of use		Sailing boat hours of use	
		Hrs/day	Total	Hrs/day	Total	Hrs/day	Total
	20	3	120	1	40	0·5	20
holiday	30 days	4	120	1·5	45	0·5	15
Working hours annually			240		85		35

This merely shows how difficult it is for a sailing boat's engine to total 100 hours working, while a motor cruiser's engine must be used very assiduously to reach 250 hours.

Sailing boats or motor sailers could allow an additional 20 hours if the annual cruise took them inland, say through the Kiel or Dutch canals. Generally speaking their engines are used only to leave harbour or for an hour or so to charge the batteries on occasional weekends.

As to motor boats, a 45-mile stretch can be covered in three hours in a semi-displacement boat that makes about 15 knots, and this is roughly equivalent to Plymouth to Torquay or Folkestone to Dunkerque, so a three-hour trip will be dependent on weather. On average between five and eight of the twenty weekends allowed for will fall through due to bad weather.

Intervals between servicing
The laborious job of analysing the servicing recommendations of twenty engine manufacturers brings such surprising results to light that, from this aspect alone, a particular engine becomes unattractive. The expert knows how much margin is allowed for safety in the periods recommended, but for the amateur this can affect his choice when buying an engine.

● Too short intervals give the impression that, for example, the rate of gas flow is much too high, i.e. the filters are inadequate. Alternatively the manufacturer has assumed that the boat owner will only carry out every alternate servicing anyway.

In the table (p. 143) three points have been extracted from maintenance recommendations, and you can see that it is not only expenditure of time that multiplies. Engine No. 2 requires 15 litres of oil and two filter cartridges more than engine No. 1, quite apart from that fact that, unless you can adjust or check the valves yourself, you have to go to a service agency and pay a very great deal of money per hour.

141

boat engines

Maintenance schedule

The maintenance schedule drawn up by the engine manufacturer is based on experience and indicates the intervals to allow between checking, maintaining and servicing the engine. Provided the engine is sensibly handled with a certain amount of sensitivity this schedule completely and entirely fulfils its purpose. At the present state of engine development the engine should run for ten years without need of repairs and should be virtually 100% reliable provided the schedule is followed exactly. The table on the next page shows the servicing intervals recommended for an engine in commercial use up to 1,000 hours of hard working, and also tabulates the annual maintenance required by a yacht engine.

It is very easy to see the difference between the intervals for the two engines with their different applications. Intervals for a boat engine cannot be based on hours of use each season; maintenance starts with fitting out after winter laying up, or even the previous autumn, for example when summer oil is replaced by an inhibiting oil that has an anti-corrosive additive but which can be left in the engine for normal working the next season.

If maintenance and care of a boat engine are to result in optimum reliability and long life they should be divided into four groups. Apart from warming up the engine as described in the chapter on handling the engine correctly these four groups can be broken down as below.

● Maintenance and care under way and when lying idle for short periods. This is really a question of listening, checking the instruments and keeping an eye on the whole installation. The more persistently that minor faults are eliminated, leakages dealt with and sight, feeling and hearing trained to respond to the engine, the more reliably will the whole installation perform.

● Lying idle for over 14 days. This is approximately the time that condensation takes to work through the film of oil on the working surfaces and into the bearings, and is why engine manufacturers recommend that some anti-corrosion measures should be taken if the interval exceeds 14 days. You may demur that it is impossible to know in advance whether, for example, a planned weekend will fall through due to bad weather. In such cases run the engine warm for at least half an hour every second weekend as a minimum. This should generally be possible even if the weather is bad.

● Laying up the engine for the winter. The yearly maintenance interval column shows very clearly what jobs must be done to protect the engine from corrosion. It would be pointless to attempt to suggest how to maintain even one major manufacturer's engines because this is given in the maintenance manual. I have omitted giving maintenance hints because, having analysed many well-known engine manufacturers' instruction manuals—and these have been very comprehensively compiled over the last few years—I consider this would only be a waste of space. As no engine instruction or maintenance manual explains why a particular job is necessary I will confine myself to the reasons in what follows.

● Fitting out the engine in the spring. This is a case of eliminating those steps that were taken to preserve the engine during the winter, and is easy enough because preservation agents today present no problems.

The whole aim of service care is to maintain the three important circuits, lubrication, cooling and fuel supply, including air. If this is done correctly, and damage to components due to wear and tear is avoided, the engine cannot help but run well. The sketch (p. 145) shows the maintenance work required. On the next pages the three circuits will be covered in turn and laying up considered. The rest will be found in your maintenance manual.

This compares two engines, one with short intervals and the other with long intervals between servicing. They are the extreme examples taken from the analysis of many maintenance schedules and instruction manuals.

MAINTENANCE WORK	Interval	Annual requirement	Time taken
Engine 1			
Oil change (5 litres)	200 hrs	5 litres oil	0·5 hrs
Oil filter cartridge	100 hrs	2 cartridges	0·5 hrs
Valve adjustment	200 hrs	once	1·0 hrs
			2·0 hrs
Engine 2			
Oil change (5 litres)	50 hrs	20 litres oil	2·0 hrs
Oil filter cartridge	50 hrs	4 cartridges	2·0 hrs
Valve adjustment	50 hrs	4 times	4·0 hrs
			8·0 hrs

This table gives the most important servicing requirements and is based on the maintenance schedule for up to 1,000 hours of heavy duty for a commercial diesel made by a well-known engine manufacturer. The interval in working hours is shown in the first column of figures and could even be doubled in normal industrial use.

As the annual hours of use in a yacht seldom exceed 200 the next two columns show yearly intervals. The last column shows which parts are subject to wear and notes after how many years replacement should be considered, or would be advisable for safety.

MAINTENANCE WORK	Interval hrs	Autumn annually	Spring annually	Wear
1 Oil change	100	x		
2 Clean and replace oil filter	100	x		
3 Oil level: injection pump, governor, gears	200	x		
4 Check vee belts	50		x	2 yrs
5 Water pumps and sea water filter	200	x		2 yrs
6 Check, clean thermostat	200			
7 Closed cooling circuit, heat exchanger	1,000			
8 Clean air filter	50	x		
9 Control cables and rods, check, grease	50	x		

boat engines

10 Fuel pre-filter, remove water, clean	200	x	x	
11 Fuel fine filter, clean, replace	500			
12 Check piping, hoses etc	50	x	x	3 yrs
13 Check valve clearances	200		x	
14 Check, tighten screws, nuts	200		x	
15 Gearbox	200	x		
16 Battery	50	as required		3 yrs
17 Alternator	1,000	lubricate		3 yrs
18 Starter motor	1,000	carbon		3 yrs
19 Check wiring	50	x	x	
20 Tank	1,000	x	x	
21 Petrol engines: carburettor and ignition	50	x	x	2 yrs

The sketch opposite shows the points which need to be checked, serviced, replaced and cleaned at certain intervals. They are so numbered that the figures relate to a continuous circuit.

First the vital functions: lubrication, without which the engine would become a wreck after only a few minutes (1–3); Vee belt (4) which drives the pumps and the alternator, Cooling circuit without which the pistons would seize up after a short time (5–7). Fuel lines without which the engine would not even start (9–11). Visual and acoustic checks (12) for wear, leaks etc.; this needs experience. Valve clearances (13) which control correct power output. Checking all nuts and bolts to be sure they are tight (14); most should only be tightened with a torque spanner. Gearbox (15), the link with the propeller. Electrical system (16–19) which provides comfort and security. Fuel tank (20), which also needs maintenance.

Petrol engines with carburettor and ignition systems need a separate chapter.

Remember the question of the size of the engine compartment as considered on p. 85 which very much decides how easy an engine is to maintain.

Protecting the engine from corrosion
As has been mentioned more than once, a boat engine suffers most when it lies idle. The build-up of condensation in the moving parts, combined with combustion deposits, attack the oil film. This can be discouraged while the boat is in the water by running the engine warm for at least half an hour every 10–14 days.

When laying up, the engine must be filled with an oil that inhibits corrosion. But that is not all; the cooling, fuel and electric circuits, as well as all other parts of the installation, must also be protected. If you are near the boat during the winter turn the propeller round a little. Condensation in the engine collects at the piston rings and eats away at the oil film there.

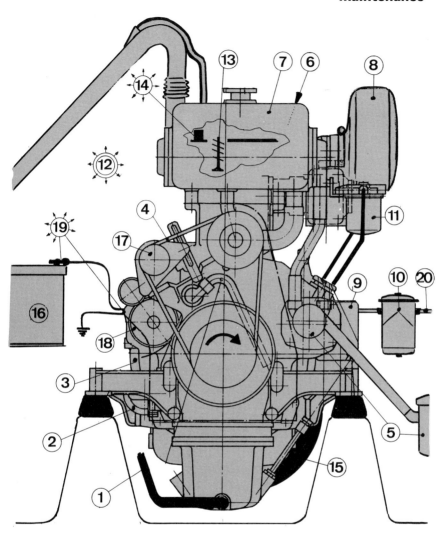

Preservation agents

For some time now all-the-year-round oil has been available, and this has anti-corrosion additives which make maintenance much easier than hitherto because the oil does not have to be rechanged in the spring. The engine can be run until the next oil change is due.

boat engines

Engines are lubricated by a pressure oil circuit; oil is sucked through the strainer (A) in the sump by the oil pump (B) and forced via the oil filter (C) through many galleries to all the lubrication points in the engine. The oil drains back into the sump and is also led there through return lines (D). The circuit is monitored by an oil pressure light or gauge. If the circuit fails and this is not noticed the engine will be wrecked within minutes and it is therefore advisable to fit an acoustic warning signal in addition to the visual oil pressure indicator. Oil that is too old is just as dangerous as lack of oil pressure, and this is why the manufacturer's oil changing intervals must be followed, as indeed must those for the oil filter and the gearbox. The whole procedure is quite simple if a sump pump is fitted to the sump drain. If wrong oil or dirty oil is used the lubricant attacks the bearings and damage is inevitable.

The gearbox has a separate oil circuit and splash lubrication is usual. The level is measured at GP while the oil is drained at GA. If the stern tube is oil-lubricated and there are other bearings these too must be dealt with in the direction indicated by SR. The figures in the engine oil circuit relate to: 1 = rocker arm lubrication. 2 = rocker arm feed. 3 = turbo-supercharger lubrication. 4 = big end bearing. 5 = crankshaft main bearing. 6 = splash lubrication for the engine spur gears; these are the gears that drive the camshaft and injection pump shafts. 7 = main oil gallery to the crankshaft bearings. 8 = camshaft bearing.

The oil filter must also be cleaned regularly in accordance with the maintenance instructions. Depending on the type of installation there is either a combined full-flow and by-flow filter or one set of filters. The by-flow filter cartridges are generally disposable. The full-flow filter, a fine mesh sieve, is washed out in petrol and reinstalled when dry or after it has been blown out. The oil should be inspected at every change, first for sludge which usually collects in the lower part of the filter. If there is a lot of grey sludge a leak in the cooling circuit should be suspected. The engine must be examined and the leak eliminated. Secondly check for slivers of metal in the oil. If there are any get expert advice. Suspended filters can easily be removed by undoing the screws, but standing filters first have to be emptied. New gaskets and O-rings should be fitted both to the sump screws and to the filter.

As well as this preservative oil for the moving parts which can be used as normal oil when the engine is running, a damp inhibiting preservative aerosol is required, also a tin of general purpose grease and, for the cooling system, cleaning and preserving fluid as approved by your engine manufacturer.

In the outboard field there has been a complete range of 'cosmetic' products for engine care and protection for years now, but this state has not yet been reached for inboard engines although market trends seem to be developing along that line. The only advice that can be given is to check in your maintenance manual. In special cases a service agency can give further advice.

Before taking the boat out of the water

In the autumn, just before the boat is taken out of the water, change the oil in the normal way, clean the filter and add fresh oil while the engine is still warm. To avoid a second change in the spring fill up with the engine oil mentioned above which is suitable for normal use as well as having anti-corrosive properties.

146

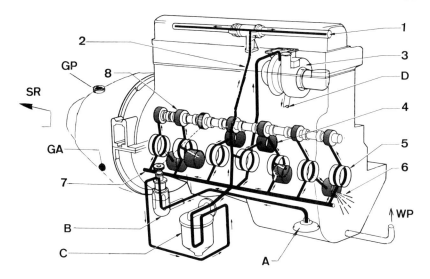

Then run the engine for a while, spray damp-inhibiting oil into the air intake after removing the air filter, — and that is all so far as the moving parts are concerned.

Cooling water system
If the engine has two circuit or indirect cooling the inner circuit should be cleaned out at least every two or three years, especially if the water that is recommended has not been used from the first. If soft water and antifreeze are used no further preservation of the inner circuit is required, and the boat can be taken out of the water.

Raw water cooling
If your engine has an open cooling circuit this must at least be rinsed out with fresh water. The sea water filter has to be dismantled and cleaned. The thermostat too should be checked every two years and the instruction manual shows how this is done. The cooling water pump is also dismantled and the impeller removed to be inspected for damage. It should not be left in the pump during the winter and will need replacing every two or three years.

Fuel circuit
Clean the filter and water separator, and vent the system. The fuel tank should either be completely emptied or filled right up to discourage condensation. If your diesel engine has pre-combustion chambers (indirect injection) these must be inspected every two or three years.

Drop in power
An inexplicable loss of power may cause you to suspect that something is

147

boat engines

wrong with the moving parts or the valves and the compression should then be checked before the boat is taken out of the water and before the oil is changed. By checking the compression pressure diagram it is easy to establish whether the piston rings are in good order and whether the valves are closing properly.

Air filter

The most unusual cause of a drop in power is the air filter which must be cleaned regularly or replaced according to its type. Three varieties of air filter are fitted to marine engines. The wet filter has a sieve-like insert which must be washed only in diesel fuel before being blown out with compressed air should this be available. When dry it is dipped in lubricating oil and can be reassembled after it has stopped dripping. Oil bath air filters, as their name implies, are immersed in an oil sump. To clean them wait a few minutes after the engine has stopped to allow the oil to settle. If the filter is too heavily clogged it must be replaced. The filter insert is washed out in diesel fuel (be careful, do not use petrol), dried, blown out with compressed air if possible, replaced in the fresh oil bath which is topped up to normal level, and reassembled. Paper filters are renewed in accordance with the manufacturer's instructions.

Daily care and maintenance

Look into the engine compartment and check everything there for leaks, wear, porous hoses, loose nuts, dust from drive belts, chafe marks etc. Deal with these immediately.

Stern-gland: oil, grease, tighten

Bilges: water?

Water separator: no water?

When the engine is running lift the cover every four hours and have a good look round.

148

6. Repairs

The moment comes when there is no way of avoiding describing something as repair work but, provided it is properly maintained, the modern boat engine needs no repairs until many years have passed.

Naturally it is not possible here to give such complete instructions that every product could be repaired, and a workshop manual fills 100 and more pages of this size for one engine. Here only the main points can be covered, as was the case with maintenance. Some points need to be thought out if a yacht is not to become a repair worskhop or store for spare parts.

A correctly maintained engine, in a sensibly conceived layout suitable for maintenance work, is not an object that sweats oily drops and is brought unwillingly to life with a spanner and a hammer, but a metal object suspended on flexible mountings that can do nothing but work if it is allowed to do so.

Far more susceptible than the engine itself are all the parts around it that can be described as ancillaries and fittings, but preventative checking and timely replacement of brittle pipes, leaking hoses, oxydised cable terminals, zinc electrodes and much more besides can hardly be described as repairs. They can all be dealt with in peace and quiet in harbour.

To get this chapter into perspective, without distorting it for better or worse through personal experience, a reasonable set of spare parts can be assembled by checking the list of spares drawn up by large manufacturers for industrial engines which are serviced regularly.

The table (p. 151) shows the spares recommended by a major manufacturer for a diesel engine, the reliability of which is acknowledged throughout the world. This table lists a set for repairs and also gives the Classification Societies' requirements for spare parts for nearer coastal work or in limited service (Lloyd's, Germanischer Lloyd, Bureau Veritas, det Norske Veritas). The last two columns again indicate my own views.

The very carefully compiled instruction manuals even show how to check valve clearances, replace an impeller, tension the vee belt and change the oil filter, all of which come under maintenance rather than repairs. When it comes to moving parts there is no alternative to taking out the engine due to lack of space. The exception is the cylinder head, but the likelihood of having to remove this without the help of a service agency is very small. Generally this only has to be done when the engine is thoroughly overhauled and moving parts, liners, piston rings etc. are replaced. Any boat making a long passage under engine

boat engines

should carry a workshop manual, and the engine manufacturer will certainly not refuse to provide one.

Even those who are not expert will realise that valve clearances must be correct. If they are too small the valves will not close properly and the correct pressure cannot be obtained for combustion—always assuming that combustion takes place at all (particularly dangerous in petrol engines). Output drops and the valve seat burns. If clearance is too great the valves do not open enough, the flow rate is reduced and scavenging of the gas mixture is adversely affected which leads to a loss of power.

Tool kit for the boat

To make a list of tools would be a waste of space because there are too many differences between the engines made by various manufacturers. Nor are the tool kits generally available sufficiently specialized. Find out for yourself what special tools and types of spanners are necessary for your engine. In principle one set of ring spanners or open-ended spanners should suffice, and these must either be metric, SAE or BS according to the country of origin of the engine. As some spanners are not widely obtainable ask your engine dealer for advice. You will also need a sparking plug spanner, screwdriver, hammer, large spanner to fit the propeller nut, one or two hacksaw blades, round file, half round file, cold chisel, wrench for the water pump, pipe wrench and pliers. Obviously the larger the vessel the more comprehensive will the tool kit be. The list given here is for a cruising boat up to about 30 ft or 9 m in length; in larger boats a separate electric circuit is required so that power tools can be carried. For a long voyage a gas blow-lamp and, sometimes, welding apparatus, vice etc. could be added. Larger yachts are often better equipped in this repsect than some service agencies on land. It is for the owner to decide how exhaustively to equip his boat, and he should not overdo it.

Spare parts

The number of spare parts carried depends on where the boat will be used, the type of engine, and how widely it is distributed.

If your boat has a marine version of an automobile or lorry engine made by a company that sells world-wide, and this is very likely to be the case up to 2×200 kW, you can assume that all those components that are common to car engines will be readily obtainable and that you will be able to find a mechanic to dismantle or fit them.

On the other hand, if you buy a 'true marine engine' or a converted vehicle engine which inevitably will not be so widely distributed, it is advisable to check whether spare parts and experienced mechanics are available to deal with any special engine problems, both in the area you plan to visit and, of course, in your home waters. The principle is to buy guaranteed spare parts and, when making longer voyages beyond the range of normal weekend and holiday trips, to assemble a suitable collection of spares in accordance with the manufacturer's advice.

The following should be carried in addition to the spare parts listed on p. 151, and the list that follows should be considered only to be a basis on which to build: reserve propeller, components for flexible couplings, packing for the stern

repairs

Column A: This is the manufacturer's small set of spares for normal commercial working (assuming that the engine is not being used at the back of beyond). This again implies that no repairs are envisaged. Column B: spare parts for main engines as specified by the Classification Societies (very out of date) for shorter coastal passages; * indicates additional spares that could be required for longer coastal passages, with twice the number of almost all other moving parts. Column C: This again is my personal opinion related to normal boat usage in European waters. If working hours are very high (over 200 hrs) oil filters and gaskets as listed in Column A should also be carried. † Only required for longer voyages under engine, and must then definitely be expanded as agreed with the engine manufacturer (e.g. impeller for cooling water pump). Warning: This list of spare parts relates only to the engine and not to the whole installation in the boat. Details of the latter will be found later.

	SPARE PARTS	2,000	4,000	6,000	A	B	C
Maintenance	Oil filter cartridge	7	14	20	2	—	1
	Gasket, oil filter	7	14	20	2	—	1
	Gasket, oil filter	7	14	20	2	—	1
	Gasket, oil filler cap	1	2	3	1	—	1
	Gasket, injector	4	8	8	4	1	2
	Gasket, cylinder head	1	2	3	1	—	1
	Gasket, hand pump	1	2	3	1	—	1
	Gasket, fuel filter	2	4	5	1	—	1
	Fuel filter insert	1	2	3	1	—	1
	Set of carbon brushes, Lima	1	2	3	1	—	1
	Set of engine gaskets	—	—	1	—	—	1
	Injector nozzle	1	1	4	1	1	1
	Drive belts	—	—	1	—	—	1
	Set of carbon brushes, starter motor	—	—	1	—	—	1
	Cooling water regulator insert	—	—	1	—	—	1
	Gaskets ⎫	7	14	20	2	—	1
	Gaskets ⎬ various	5	10	15	2	—	1
	Gaskets ⎭	5	10	15	2	—	1
	Pressure pipe for one cylinder	—	—	1	—	1	1
Repairs	Inlet valve	—	—	4	—	1	†
	Exhaust valve	—	—	4	—	2	†
	Valve spring	—	—	8	—	2	†
	Cylinder head	—	—	1	—	—*	†
	Set of piston rings	—	—	4	—	1*	†
	Small end bushing	—	—	1	—	1	†
	Connecting rod bolt	—	—	8	—	1	†

151

boat engines

tube (warning! do not replace while the boat is afloat), zinc anodes, set of sparking plugs if you have a petrol engine, shear pins, shaft key if required for the propeller shaft, propeller nut (also for propellers with friction coupling), gaskets for the sea water filter, water separator, sea-cock, air filter inserts where applicable, set of gaskets for the fuel pumps unless these are included in the set of engine gaskets, ignition cable, distributor rotor arm for petrol engines, lubricant and preservative agents (damp-inhibiting oil in aerosol container), sea-water resistant and general purpose grease, enough engine and gearbox oil for one change (only for longer voyages), grease gun if the engine has grease nipples.

For emergency repairs: a few metres of copper wire about 1 mm in diameter, adhesive tape, insulating tape, hose clips (various, stainless), flexible cable (single core 1·5 sq.mm cross-sectional area), rubber rings cut from motor car tyres, rubber strops with plastic hooks, a few short pieces of copper tubing, of the same size as the various fuel and cooling water lines, to use as connecting pieces in an emergency.

Always work on the principle that

● spare parts are only useful if they have not become unserviceable when stored. Grease them and wrap them in protective foil.

● The Classification Societies' recommendations are of very limited value so far as yachts are concerned because they relate too much to large ships' machinery. The interior of a yacht engine is only accessible when the engine is taken out and turned round or removed entirely.

● It cannot really be considered sensible to carry no spare parts on the basis that 'I could not repair it myself anyway'. It is often easier to find a skilled mechanic than the parts required.

152

Quantity	Multiply number of	by	To obtain number of	Multiply number of	by	To obtain number of
Length	inches	25·4	mm	mm	·0393701	inches
	inches	2·54	cm	cm	·393701	inches
	inches	·0254	metres	metres	39·3701	inches
	feet	·3048	metres	metres	3·28084	feet
Area	sq. inches	6·4516	cm²	cm²	·155	sq. inches
	sq. feet	·092903	m²	m²	10·763916	sq. feet
Volume	inches³	·016387	dm³ (litre)	dm³ (litre)	61·02399	inches³
	feet³	·0283168	m³	m³	35·31473	feet³
	gallons	4·54609	dm³ (litre)	dm³ (litre)	·219969	gallons
Mass	lbs	·45359237	kg	kg	2·20462	lbs
	tons	1·01605	tonnes (1,000 kg)	tonnes	·984203	tons (2,240 lbs)
Velocity	feet/min	0·00508	m/sec	m/sec	196·8504	feet/min
	knots (Br)	0·514772	m/sec	m/sec	1·942608	knot (Br)
	knots (Br)	1·8531792	km/hour	km/hour	·539613	knot (Br)
	knots (Int)	0·514444	m/sec	m/sec	1·943846	knot (Int)
	knots (Int)	1·852	km/hour	km/hour	·539957	knot (Int)
	km/hour	·277778	m/sec	m/sec	3·6	km/hour
Force	lbf	4·44822	N	N	·224809	lbf
	kgf	9·80665	N	N	1·019716	kgf
	lbf	·4535922	kgf	kgf	2·2046234	lbf
Torque	lbf. ft	1·35582	Nm	Nm	·737561	lbf. ft
	kgf. m	9·80665	Nm	Nm	1·019716	kgf. m
	kgf. m	7·233029	lbf. ft	lbf. ft	·138255	kgf. m

Quantity	From	Factor	To	Factor	To
Force / Area	lbf/inch²	6894·76	N/m²	·0001450377	lbf.inch²
	lbf/inch²	·689476	n/cm²	1·450377	lbf/inch²
	lbf/inch²	·0689476	bar	14·50377	lbf/inch²
Power	horsepower (Br)	·7457	kW	1·341022	hp (Br)
	horsepower (m)	·735499	kW	1·359621	hp (metric)
	hp (metric)	·98632	hp (British)	1·01387	hp (metric)
Power to weight ratio	$\dfrac{\text{lbs}}{\text{hp (Br)}}$	·6082781	$\dfrac{\text{kg}}{\text{kW}}$	1·6439849	$\dfrac{\text{lbs}}{\text{hp (Br)}}$
Fuel consumption	gal/kWh	4·54609	litres/kWh	·219969	gal/kWh
Speed to length ratio	$\dfrac{\text{knots}}{\text{ft}}$	3·35	$\dfrac{\text{km/h}}{\text{m}}$	·298	$\dfrac{\text{knots}}{\text{ft}}$
Power to volume ratio	$\dfrac{\text{hp (Br)}}{\text{in}^3}$	45·505583 (45·5)	$\dfrac{\text{kW}}{\text{litre}}$	·0219753 (0·22)	$\dfrac{\text{hp (Br)}}{\text{in}^3}$

SI prefixes: micro, $=10^{-6}$: milli (m) $=10^{-3}$: centi (c) $=10^{-2}$:
deci (c) $=10^{-1}$: deca (da) $=10^{1}$: kilo (k) $=10^{3}$
Mega (M) $=10^{6}$

Named units: Newton (force) : Joule (work and heat) : Watt (power) :
Pascal (pressure $= \dfrac{\text{Newton}}{\text{metre}^2}$)

Constants

ABLE SIZES AND RATINGS (Copies from Perkins' marine installation know-how)
Lloyds Requirements

Number and diameter inches of strands comprising the conductor	Nominal Cross-sectional area of stranded conductor inches²	mm²	Rubber or PVC Insulation 1 core	2 core	Butyl Insulation 1 core	2 core	Mineral Insulation 1 core	2 core	Resistance for 1 foot of conductor (Ohms)
1/·044	0·0015	0·97	9	7	15	12	19	16	0·00547
3/·029	0·002	1·3	11	9	19	16	23	19	0·00428
3/·036	0·003	1·94	14	11	23	19	27	23	0·00275
7/·029	0·0045	2·9	18	16	29	24	34	29	0·00183
7/·036	0·007	4·5	25	21	38	32	44	37	0·00118
7/·044	0·01	6·5	31	26	48	40	56	47	0·00079
7/·052	0·0145	9·3	37	31	60	51	70	59	0·00056
7/·064	0·225	14·5	51	43	78	66	93	79	0·00037
9/·044	0·03	19·4	60	51	93	79	110	93	0·00029
9/·052	0·04	20·6	72	61	115	96	135	115	0·00027
9/·064	0·06	38·7	92	78	145	120	175	150	0·00014

Formula to calculate the cross-sectional area of the conductor

Cross-sectional Area of conductor (mm²) =

$$\frac{\text{Length of conductor (m)}^* \times \text{Current (amperes)}}{56^* \times \text{Drop in voltage (V)}\dagger}$$

* 56 = copper conductor: length of conductor = twice cable length
† 2% for navigation lights: 5% for other equipment

Index

157

index